All I Know About Animal Behavior I Learned in Loehmann's Dressing Room

Books by Erma Bombeck

At Wit's End

"Just Wait Till You Have Children of Your Own!"

I Lost Everything in the Post-Natal Depression

The Grass Is Always Greener Over the Septic Tank

If Life Is a Bowl of Cherries, What Am I Doing in the Pits?

Aunt Erma's Cope Book

Motherhood: The Second Oldest Profession

Family: The Ties That Bind . . . and Gag!

I Want to Grow Hair, I Want to Grow Up,
I Want to Go to Boise

When You Look Like Your Passport Photo,
It's Time to Go Home

A Marriage Made in Heaven . . . Or Too Tired for an Affair

All I Know About Animal Behavior I Learned in
Loehmann's Dressing Room

ERMA BOMBECK

All I Know About Animal Behavior I Learned in Loehmann's Dressing Room

HarperCollins*Publishers*

HarperCollins books may be purchased for educational, business, or sales promotional use. For information please write: Special Markets Department, HarperCollins Publishers, Inc., 10 East 53rd Street, New York, NY 10022.

FIRST EDITION

Designed by Nancy Singer

Library of Congress Cataloging-in-Publication Data

Bombeck, Erma.
    All I know about animal behavior I learned in Loehmann's dressing room/Erma Bombeck.
       p.   cm.
    ISBN 0-06-017788-8
       1. Man—Animal nature—Humor.   2. Animal behavior—Humor.
    3. Human behavior—Humor.   I. Title.
    PS3552.O59A77   1995
    814'.54—dc20   95-36835

95 96 97 98 99 ❖/RRD 10 9 8 7 6 5 4 3 2 1

*To all the animals I exploited in this book who won't
see a dime of the profits*

*To Norma Born, my secretary, who lists the library
as her home address on her driver's license*

All I Know About
Animal Behavior
I Learned
in Loehmann's
Dressing Room

Introduction

In the sixties when Jane Goodall was in Africa studying the behavior of chimpanzees in the wild, I was in Centerville, Ohio, keeping vigil over three children under age five.

Not a day went by that I didn't question why I was chosen to monitor the daily habits of a trio of drooling *Homo sapiens* while Jane was in shorts working on her tan.

From time to time, I would see her on PBS, and for days afterward, I would fantasize about climbing to a solitary hill to watch chimps pick and eat bugs off their siblings.

No pantyhose riding around my hips, no fight with the traffic every day, no kids pounding "Heart and Soul" on the piano for five hours nonstop, no going through the garbage looking for a sales slip. I would just sit there quietly while some chimpanzee stomped his brother's face into the dirt and smile and say, "I'd intercede, but it would flaw my research."

Jane and I met only once and I was beside myself with admiration. I think she said to me, "Aren't you curious as to whether or not the chimps have a sense of humor?" and I replied, "If I had a face like that, I know I would."

I didn't begin to convey the respect I had for the work she was doing or my disappointment that I had squandered my life scrutinizing the behavior of humans. For nearly thirty years I have recorded essays of people's mating habits, maternal instincts, and reproductive cycles; of how they handle trends and technology; of what makes them laugh and what makes them cry.

But I had not produced the breakthrough for which I had hoped.

One day as I was shuffling through the newspaper, I saw a picture of an elephant named Lucille from our local zoo. Lucille had a paintbrush in her trunk and was splashing and dribbling colors onto the canvas like a drunken house painter. The painting sold for $250.

The picture dredged up memories of a routine by comedian Jonathan Winters, who drew an irregular circle on a piece of paper with a small line coming out of the top. He labeled it "Christmas ornament" and put a price tag of $4,000 on it. It always got big laughs.

Lucille had to be the first stand-up comic in the animal kingdom and no one realized it.

The breakthrough hit me like a bolt. Jane and I were studying the same species. Maybe some of them had more fur, fewer teeth, longer tails, and more interesting sex lives, but the correlation was there. Some of us were more poorly engineered than others (bats have tits located under their armpits), but generally, humans are not that far apart from bush animals. We share the same planet, breathe the same air, and sometimes vie for the same food. We certainly have the same goal—survival.

Consider the camel. He has yellow teeth, corns, and halitosis. When he catches a cold he mopes around with his nose running and is unbelievably rude. Now don't tell me you haven't had a blind date who matches that description perfectly.

Sometimes we even resemble one another. I once worked for a woman with a face like a ferret. It would not have surprised me if she burrowed into a hole at night.

On the following pages is a look at how close animals in the wild and humans really are.

An African monkey supposedly is adept at picking every lock on every cage he has been in. For that he got twenty minutes on a *National Geographic* special. I had a cousin with the same skill who got two years.

We can learn a lot from one another. The hippopotamus is a vegetarian and looks like a wall. Lions who eat only red meat are sleek and slim. Could it be that human nutritionists are on the wrong track?

The gap closes daily. It will be only a matter of time before humans become smart enough to attach a beeper collar to their teenagers to track where they go and what they do once they get there.

So which animal is smarter? The wild female Virginia

opossum who produces up to fifty babies yet has only thirteen teats, or the human female who gives birth to three offspring and has only two windows in the backseat of her car?

Think about it.

1

The female African elephant carries her baby for a period of 660 days before giving birth. The infant weighs three hundred pounds and is born with stretch marks. The female nurses it for three years and continues breeding until she is ninety years old.

Before you get too choked up about the 660-day gestation period of an elephant, you have to know that in human terms it comes out to about nine months.

You also have to consider that elephants are tall. You can get by carrying three hundred extra pounds if you are tall enough to eat branches off a thirty-foot tree. I have always believed that women under five feet, eight inches should never carry a child. They look dumpy.

I do know that things have changed for pregnant women. Human pregnancies used to be a fun time for women. Oh sure, you were carrying around a watermelon seed inside of you that grew to the size of a piano, but there were no diet restrictions, you were actually advised to give up exercise, it was all right to drink coffee or alcohol, you could soak up sun on the beach, and people treated you with all the care and vigilance of a homemade time bomb.

There was a mystique about the condition. You were doing something that no man had ever done or could do in the history of civilization.

Then carrying a baby became ordinary. Everyone was doing it. Women ran marathons in the eighth month, a female jockey gave birth just hours after riding her third horse of the day, anchorwomen signed off the six o'clock news with contractions coming every three minutes. I remember reading that Marla Maples (who eventually became Mrs. Donald Trump) had to pull out of a Broadway show, *The Will Rogers Follies,* because her pregnancy interfered with her cartwheels. (She is tall.)

Experts decreed that exercise was good for you, sun was bad, coffee and alcohol were no-no's, and you had to watch your weight gain and eat sensibly.

It wasn't fun anymore.

During the first few months, people were excited for you. Their response to your condition was a universal one.

They would stare at your stomach and say, "You don't even look pregnant." (Why would you when you were carrying an object no bigger than a comma?)

At four months as you struggled to keep in civilian clothes, they would say as one, "You're pregnant, all right." (Well, it wasn't a big lunch!)

At six months, the general consensus is, "Are you sure there's just one in there?" (As compared to what? A litter?)

It's at eight and a half months that the mood turns impatient. "Haven't you had that baby yet?"

For me it was especially sensitive when the baby was a year old and they were still asking, "Haven't you had that baby yet?"

It was the baby boomers who got creative with the birthing process.

For a generation who couldn't wait for paint to dry or a light to turn green, they didn't even have the patience to wait a month or two to make sure they were pregnant. They discovered they could pee on a little strip of paper and if it turned pink or another happy color, they could start shopping for a nanny. They wanted to know the sex of the child before it was born. No one knows why this is important or what they do with the information, but they wanted to know.

The old joke, "Are you pregnant?" followed by, "No, I'm carrying it for a friend," became a reality. Surrogate mothers are having babies for women unable to have their own.

Frozen embryos have become something to fight over at the divorce, along with the Chicago Bulls season tickets. It gives new meaning to the question, "Daddy, where did I come from?" ("You were thawed in Milwaukee, son.")

To improve on the genetics you married, sperm banks came into being. You can make your selection as if you are ordering carry-out. "I'll have one Nobel physicist, hold the poet laureate, and a concert violinist on the side."

Baby boomers even created their own timetable. At one time, if you didn't have a baby by the age of forty, you couldn't give your biological clock away at a garage sale.

They changed all that. A fifty-nine-year-old woman in Great Britain who was artificially impregnated gave birth to twins. Another mother carried her own twin grandchildren for her daughter, who was unable to have her own.

It's just my opinion, but giving birth at this advanced age can't go much farther. Having a delivery covered by Medicare just isn't going to fly. It's too risky for a woman to put a baby down and not remember where she left it.

In a society where it's a big deal to get men to pour water into an electric coffee machine in the morning, you cannot help but be impressed at the progress made in reproduction in the animal kingdom.

Several species of male animals actually give birth. This is wonderful. For years, women have felt guilty for not sharing with men the exhilaration of a fetal foot that kicks the book out of their hands or the challenge of trying to turn over in bed with the equivalent of a twenty-pound bag of bird food taped to their stomachs.

The female seahorse, for example, places her eggs in a womblike pouch on the male seahorse's belly. It is his belly that swells during pregnancy and goes through the powerful contractions to bring forth the newborn.

The male bell toad hasn't quite gone that far, but he's on his way to greatness. The female lays a string of eggs three to four feet long, which the two-inch male struggles to wrap around his body like a huge sash. For over a month he lugs this load about, hiding during the day and dragging himself to the stream at night to moisten the eggs. When they finally hatch, the exhausted father gratefully watches the tiny tadpoles swim away.

He remains silent for the rest of the year, possibly from fatigue.

It doesn't have to be like that. If he'd grow a little taller, things would be easier.

Next to having the male species carry the babies, my vote for the perfect child-bearing mother would be the giraffe. At twenty-three feet tall, she could be carrying a Land Rover around in her stomach, and who would know? She doesn't even lie down to have her baby. She simply stops, and the baby falls five or six feet to the ground like a cement delivery.

There are as many ways and length of terms to propagate the species as there are mothers or fathers. Bats mate upside down, humans on TV, but one trend seems to be closing the gap. Due to fertility drugs, humans are having litters. There is not a day you don't pick up the paper and read that someone just gave birth to four, five, or six babies.

A story in the *New York Times* revealed that with a few physical adjustments, men could give birth.

I just hope the seahorse hasn't talked too much.

2

Paper training a mature dog requires the owner to have breakfast sitting with him in a small room and waiting for him to urinate. It may take hours.

If you're a mother, you've been there watching your kid sit on the potty unraveling toilet tissue. If they were like mine, they were twenty-three years old before they realized the sky didn't have a light and an exhaust fan in it.

It was like an arms race in which you wanted to be the first on your block to lose the diapers and get on with your life.

Well, Yogi Berra was right. "It ain't over till it's over." The whole revelation started with June Allyson, who daringly admitted on a television commercial that a lot of older men and women out there weren't having fun sitting for days with their legs crossed. They had lost their bladder control and needed diapers. What goes around comes around.

The mature bladder that was once capable of lasting through *A Chorus Line* (which has no intermission) now found it couldn't wait for a bathroom if there was a stop sign between your front door and your car.

The explanation for a toddler's not being able to control his bladder was that the muscles weren't developed yet. The explanation for an older person's not being able to control the bladder was that it was hanging around the knees and had no elasticity left.

More and more commercials began to appear with a solution to the problem. They usually were aired during the dinner hours between ads for burning hemorrhoids and yeast infections.

Before you regress to Pampers, a doctor who is aware of the problem prescribes exercise. Exercise is the present-day penicillin of the medical profession. You can't see well? Exercise your eye muscles. You can't walk steadily? Exercise your leg muscles. You can't hold your pee-pee? Exercise whatever is left down there.

Sometimes they can take a tuck and right the problem, but June Allyson seems to have the simplest solution.

It's an inconvenience you can usually spot. Look for the woman stopping the car suddenly and aiming for a Porta-Potty at a construction site.

Keep your eye on the woman who pulls into a handicapped spot, doesn't lock the car, and heads for the physically challenged booth in the restroom, which is not usually in use.

A woman has a problem when she hears the overture and leaves to go to the bathroom.

Another giveaway is when all the kids are in the car and Grandma says, "Oh well, just one more for the road," and ducks into the powder room.

If I had known toilet training wasn't forever and would recur in another forty-seven years, I'd have done things differently. I wouldn't have made those ridiculous promises to the kids like, "Go toi-toi for Mommy and I'll let you drive Daddy's car."

I certainly wouldn't have made dustcloths out of all those diapers.

I heard a bladder control commercial the other day that pointed out a woman could now jump in the air without worry. Women that age usually don't have too much to get airborne over.

None of this is funny to the women who walk around with leaky plumbing. I just find it ironic that the woman who can't pass a restroom ends up in a doctor's toilet with an empty specimen cup because she can't go.

Tell me about it. I'm the woman who once sat on the edge of a bathtub for thirty-six hours pleading with my toddler, "Sweetheart, does the word 'deliverance' have any meaning for you?"

3

Four bottlenose dolphins were trapped by ice in the Shrewsbury River near Sea Bright, New Jersey. The dolphins, noted for their extraordinary radar system, obviously took a wrong turn and swam south when they should have gone north to the Atlantic Ocean.

I have just come up with a wonderful solution to end all wars. Let men give directions on how to get there.

There is no species on the face of this earth that prides itself more on how to get around than men. Yet most of them are lost their entire lifetimes. They just won't admit it.

I can always tell when my husband is lost. He starts to dispense guilt. "Are you sure you read the route number right?" And, as we're knee-deep in farm animals staring in our windows, "Did AAA say anything about a detour?"

If you really want to set a man off, tell him to stop and ask someone where you are.

"Why should I do that?" he asks.

"Because we are lost."

"I am not lost. I just made a wrong turn."

"Same thing. We have passed this gas station three times."

"That's a good thing. At least it's familiar."

To stop and ask someone for directions is to compromise his masculinity.

Despite the fact that men don't have a clue where they are most of the time, they insist on giving directions to women—a process better known as death by instruction.

I am standing at the door with my car keys in my hand when he says, "Do you know where you're going?"

"Yes."

"I thought not," he says, putting down his paper. "You go west on Silver Street for two blocks and then turn north until you reach the freeway. At the freeway, go east and . . ."

Now that drives me crazy. He knows I don't speak compass. Unless you're talking about the Civil War, north and south have no meaning for me. North is always opposite my right hand and south my left, no matter which way I'm standing. The same with miles. I walked a mile once and it was the longest hour and a half I ever spent, so forget miles.

"Tell me right or left," I beg.

"I have tried giving you directions in left and right," he says patiently.

"And?"

"You have gotten lost. Let me draw you a map."

"Oh Lord, forget it. Just tell me when I get to the end of the street, which way do I turn?"

"North . . . rather, right. Then turn right again and if you are blinded by the sun you are going in the wrong direction."

"I always thought the sun came up in the east."

"Not at 4:30 in the afternoon," he says dryly.

"Why do you always try to confuse me? I think you do that to make yourself feel important."

"Why can't you have a little patience?" he asks.

"At my age, patience is not a virtue . . . it's a luxury."

Wherever lost women gather—at service stations, in obscure cornfields, and on exit ramps—we talk about this thing men have about giving directions.

One woman told an unbelievable story one day about being lost. She stopped at a service station and said, "I am trying to find where my son's baseball team is practicing. I'm looking for Prindle's Field."

The man stroked his chin and said, "Prindle's Field is about three miles west of Dake's Corners off the Hans Expressway using the Mill Road exit.

"You go by two stop signs, make a right at the overhead, and there's a church on the corner that used to be Presbyterian but was bought out by the Methodists. You take a jog in the road and follow through to a dead end, then turn left and you'll see a little filling station called Fred's."

She looked up and observed, "That's the name of this station. Where's Prindle's Field?"

"That's what I'm getting around to telling you. You're there. It's behind the station."

The male species has a superiority complex about driving. I wish I had a dime for every joke about woman drivers I've been assaulted with. They relish telling about the woman in driving school who consistently flunked her test because she couldn't be sure which was her right hand and which was her left.

Years later she met her old driving instructor, who asked if she ever figured it out.

"Certainly," she said proudly. "I drive every day now." She held up both hands. "Ruby ring, right, and diamond ring, left."

Women have their jokes on men who drive. My favorite is: If a man and a woman jumped off a building at the same time, who would reach the ground first? Answer? The woman. The man would get lost.

Douglas Corrigan never asked for directions. He just announced to a crowd of reporters and cameras in 1938 that he was headed for California, hopped into his monoplane, and to the horror of the people on the ground, made a wide circle and ended up in Dublin, Ireland.

Roy Riegels never asked. He was the USC center who was pitted against Georgia in the Rose Bowl game in 1929. When a Georgia player fumbled, Riegels came up with the ball and started a dash to the goal line. Unfortunately, it was the wrong one. His own man finally stopped him on the three-yard line.

And while we're talking heroes, Christopher Columbus wasn't all that swift. Turn the guy around in the Bahamas a couple of times and he couldn't find America if it was on fire.

You can say what you want about women's lack of direction, but it was a man who was found by a police officer recently, sitting in his car alongside Interstate 8 where it stops at Ocean Beach in San Diego.

He had a map in his lap and a perplexed look on his face. The motorist told the officer he had come from New Mexico and was looking for Arizona. He said he must have missed it.

I don't care what they say about animals having great sonar powers and whales showing up in the Baja every year. How do we know they want to go to Mexico? For all we know, they were headed for Hawaii but the male was too proud to ask directions.

4

*Prairie dogs are social animals who greet one
another by sniffing, snuggling, and kissing.*

I have been saying hello and good-bye for a lot of years
and I still don't have the hang of it.

No matter how hard I try, I still cannot figure out
who kisses, who shakes hands, who hugs, and who just
waves or nods.

Every time I think I'm saying hello to a shaker, he's
invariably a hugger, and I end up with my arms stiff at
my sides, looking like a mummy who has just fallen out
of the case.

On the other hand, if he's a kisser and I think he's a
waver, I end up with my hand in his ear.

All I know is, you can't just say, "Hi, how's it going?"
Nearly everyone today puckers and pecks.

People eating lunch will hurriedly wipe crumbs from
their mouths and bury their faces in your hair to finish

the job. Visitors to the sick in hospitals lean over long, pale, lifeless forms in little short gowns, and God knows what they're embracing.

The most awkward greeting is the Catholic Church's kiss of peace during the Mass. At one point in the service, the congregation is asked to turn to the people around them and offer a wish for peace, sometimes accompanied by a hug or a kiss. It's like a religious blind date.

I was never surprised when my children assumed a fetal position under the kneeler when this occurred.

For sheer drama, however, nothing compares to the talk show kiss-up. The first encounter with the host is usually in the makeup room, where you greet each other with an enthusiastic hug and kiss. Later in the green room, you encounter those who will be joining you on the show and there is another round of embraces and cheek-pecking.

When you finally emerge from behind the curtain to take your place in the hot seat, you express surprise at seeing the host whom you saw five minutes ago and kiss the air near his cheek so your makeup and hair will remain intact. You do the same for each guest.

At the end of the show, everyone stands up and proceeds to kiss one another good-bye . . . unless you meet them again in the parking lot.

Not everyone is comfortable with the kissing ritual. My husband is one of them. He refuses to press lips with anyone except his wife, mother, and dog. If someone wanted to give him mouth-to-mouth resuscitation, he would refuse until he had been formally introduced.

He regards kissing as a clearinghouse for germs and wants no part of it. When he is confronted by a social kisser, he stands with his arms hanging limply by his sides and his body erect. It's like making a pass at a food blender.

Kissing on television has become as exciting as watching someone wolf down a late lunch.

Couples work so hard at something that should be relaxed and pleasurable. Body parts that I cannot identify flip across the screen and masses of hair literally cover the bed. I know they're young, but I've become so practical about it that when one of their heads hangs over the bed, I yell at the set, "The back! Support the back."

I saw a Western the other night in which the hero had been left to die in the desert. His beard was long, his clothes were dusty, and he hadn't brushed or flossed since heaven knows when. He had also been without food. The heroine jumped from her horse, ran over, and kissed him passionately on the mouth. Puleeese. When beef jerky comes in, love goes right out the window.

Let us not forget the animals who can't say good-bye.

In 1939, a coast guard vessel was cruising the Canadian Arctic when the men spotted a polar bear on an ice floe. What a novelty for the seamen, who threw it salami, peanut butter, and chocolate bars. Then they ran out of the food. The polar bear hadn't run out of appetite, so he proceeded to board the vessel. The men on ship were terrified and opened the fire hoses on him. The polar bear loved it and raised his paws in the air to get the water under his armpits. He was eventually forced to return to his ice pad.

My Uncle Kenneth was less dramatic. When he and my aunt would come for a visit to the house I would say, "Aunt Louise, I think Uncle Kenneth is ready to go home."

"How can you tell?" she asked.

"He's in the car, the motor is turning over, and your car is slowly backing out of the driveway."

No blowing of a kiss, no "I had a nice time," no handshake, no "We'll keep in touch."

It seems to be a guy thing. Men don't hang around for small talk; they just split. A woman, on the other hand, has a need for closure. As she stands at the door, she will tell you how great it was seeing you again and how you should get together more often. She will make plans to call next week. You'll hug on the average of five times before she assures you, "You really *do* look wonderful" and says, "Promise you'll call."

When you walk her to her car, you hang on to the door for another ten minutes and run alongside the vehicle like a Secret Service agent guarding the president.

Women are sometimes awkward about touchy-feely, but it is something that seems to be expected. It's hard to do what our mothers used to say we'd go blind for if we weren't married. Touching with affection now is an acceptable part of our society.

We all stumble through it somehow, but I *was* secretly impressed with the woman who was leaving a party recently. The host reached out to kiss her and she said, "I have a cold." He started to hug her and she said, "I have a bad back."

When he reached out to shake her hand, she said, "Sorry, too many rings." When he waved, she grinned. "I have a jealous husband."

Then she turned and winked. "But write me."

It is clearly a custom that needs rules. Without them, we are going to have a lot of stepping on feet, bumping noses, getting hair caught in braces, having glasses lock, lipstick appearing in strange places, and general confusion.

These are my suggestions:

1. Read the name tag—if one exists—to know whom you're kissing.

2. Make a quick appraisal of things that hurt—pens, credit cards with sharp edges, key rings, packages, and sprayed hair. Approach with caution.

3. With arms outstretched, tell the kissee he or she looks wonderful.

4. Step forward with your right foot to maintain balance and firmly grasp the other's hand and aim for the left side of the face. *Left!* That's important.

5. Pucker your lips, close your eyes (to avoid foreign objects striking you blind), and try not to make direct contact with the cheek or lips.

6. Whisper, "We must get together again soon."

Experts in the field of humanistic psychology concede that many people hug and are very conscious of the importance of touch. It helps people feel good about themselves, aids in the healing process, and relieves stress.

Kissing has become a habit with me. I kiss everybody. I kissed the man who changed the thermostat in my oven the other day. I was genuinely glad to see him, okay?

5

The wildebeest is an animal of great drive. He will travel eight hundred miles to get to where he wants to go. He will throw himself off riverbanks, swim rivers infested with crocodiles, endure floods and enemies to get to his destination. There is no stopping him on his annual migration.

Los Angeles is having an earthquake that registers 6.6 on the Richter scale. A woman in her car is frantic as she is turned back by a policeman who advises her that the freeway ahead of her has crumbled. Feverishly, she puts her car in reverse and winds in and out of back roads and streets littered with glass and debris, observing small fires, people wandering the streets dazed, and emergency vehicles with lights illuminating the devastation.

Finally, she pulls into a small strip shopping center, walks through the door of her beauty shop, and says, "Sorry I'm late, Pierre."

A woman who is a "standing" at the beauty shop can make a postman look like a shut-in. When you talk about snow, rain, heat, and the gloom of night, you're talking about a woman who puts her hair appointment above life itself.

Disasters are nothing more than challenges to her. She will commandeer a rowboat in a flood to drop off for a blow-dry. She will grope and stumble in the darkness of brownouts.

The only concession she makes during an earthquake is an instruction to "Hold the manicure until the shock waves pass."

In Nome, Alaska, where you would imagine beauty shops would close their doors during the deep freeze, women climb into their cars with square tires and solid fuel lines and inch their way through blizzards of eighty degrees below zero to get their roots touched up.

There are certain things a woman simply cannot do with dirty hair. She cannot give birth, be married, drop off a child in public, stay at the scene of an accident, or answer the phone with her husband's old girlfriend on the line.

One of the first appointments a new widow makes upon hearing her husband has died is with her hairdresser. At the funeral she may look like roadkill, but every hair is in place and sprayed to stay there until the end of the century.

The lousier I feel, the more determined I am that it is because it's a bad hair day. I have been known to hang over the toilet bowl and lose my lunch, and when my husband presses a cold, wet cloth to my head, I jerk it away, throw it on the floor, and snap, "You fool! You're taking the curl out of my hair."

I know whatever I have I will never get well if my hair is greasy. That's a fact.

I also know that hair will grow at an astonishing rate when you are incapacitated. Bangs can grow as much as six inches in one week, and short hair that started at the nape of your neck will cascade over your pillow in three days. You don't want to know what happens to your roots.

Once a woman becomes a "standing" and has an appointment with destiny every week of her life, the habit is impossible to break.

A few years ago I had an occasion to visit the Soviet Union for a few weeks. I had my hair combed out moments before boarding the plane so it would be "fresh." However, five days later I realized it was time for damage control.

Despite the fact that I knew only two Russian words—caviar and Gorbachev—I pantomimed my way into a Russian full-service spa.

Communication with your own hairdresser at best is like breaking the Navajo code in World War II. You learn things. You learn never to say, "Just take a little off" to a man who buys shampoo by the case and cotton by the bale. You learn that ripping out a picture of Julia Roberts and holding it in front of him and saying, "It's me" is risky. If he bends over in laughter and has to leave the room, put it away for some other time. "Surprise me" is a phrase that should never be used. I don't have to explain that, do I?

Back to the Russian spa. The hairdresser had thirty pounds of hair that looked like an unmade bed. That should have tipped me off. I began slowly drawing pictures with my hands. "A pouf here with a wave over the ear and this glob goes back and is swirly and this bunch of hair can go choo choo choo into a bang. Okay?"

She stood poised with her comb. Neither moved.

I repeated the directions.

Finally, she moved to her countertop and held up a picture of Linda Evans. Linda Evans had shoulder-length blond hair. My hair was nothing more than a mouse-brown beanie that covered my head with a three-inch bang.

I smiled. "Perfect."

She grabbed the scissors and began snipping away, smiling and humming. When she handed me the mirror to see what she had done, she said in flawless English, "It'll grow out."

It's the universal language of hairdressers.

Men have never understood the bond that exists between women and their hairdressers. They do not consider hair one of the major religions. If their hair meets their coat collar and zings in nine different directions, they have no urgency whatsoever to have it trimmed. They say, "I need a haircut" in the same tone as they say, "I need change for the coffee machine." There is no communication between them and their barber. They sit in a chair and read a newspaper, close their eyes when they are gassed with powder, pay their bill, and leave. Some don't even bother to see what has been done to them.

It's a girl thing. The migration to the beauty shop will not be deterred by a dead car battery, inclement weather, an empty gas tank, a sitter who doesn't show, or a direct hit on the shop by a bomb.

A person has been known to come between a mother and child and live—but don't even think of keeping a woman away from her hairdresser.

6

When a white-tailed deer was hurt, a vet cleaned the wounded area with carbolic water and bandaged it. The deer darted away, pulled the bandage off, licked the wound, exposed it to the sunlight, and healed himself.

Never has there been such an interest in alternative medicine. It spans a spectrum that goes from biofeedback and herbs to meditation and acupuncture; from tai chi to diets of shark cartilage to treat cancer; from support groups to "Put your hands on the radio, Billie Joe, and say hallelujah."

All of it is speculative, but many people are turning to it because of their bizarre excursions through traditional medicine.

We have all been there. When I'm sick, the first thing the medical profession does is order me out of my bed and into the office where they dress me in a Hefty Bag and put me on a cold table. They give me a copy of *Cysts Digest* to read while I'm waiting. The doctor arrives and asks, "What seems to be your problem?"

I tell him I'm not happy with my life, all my appliances are going, and I need dental work. I'm talking back to bumper stickers. My hair doesn't shine anymore and I've had to change door keys on my kids three times.

"You should be depressed," he says. "That's not a flattering dress." Then he proceeds to write a prescription for a drug that costs more than my winter utility bill.

The second thing the medical profession is good at is matching you up with a medical blind date. They put you in a sterile hospital room with a person you have never met before. Roommates are often at different stages of recovery. If you draw someone who is eating nacho chips and yells out the answers to *Jeopardy!* questions on the TV and all you want to do is throw up, this could be a problem. There is a correlation between how sick you are and how many visitors your roommate entertains. The worse you feel, the more traffic.

Traditional medicine decrees you should never be left alone in the hospital. There is a steady stream of strangers who wander in demanding blood and urine samples and are never seen again.

There are nutritionists who take it personally that you did not eat all your lima beans. There's a group of doctors who are "in training" and look at you like they're going to be ill.

In between all the company, there are a myriad of tests. There is a great demand for these tests, and most of your time is spent on a cart in a basement hallway somewhere staring at the ceiling. The only thing you can count on is that if the test requires them to fill you up to capacity with something until you cannot take it anymore, the bathroom is in the east wing and you are in the west wing.

My personal favorite is the MRI (magnetic resonance imaging). This is a sophisticated X ray that requires your body to be stuffed into a small cylinder the size of a toilet tissue roll. Once I am in there with my arms to my side cursing the darkness, a voice piped in from a booth nearby asks, "Are you claustrophobic, Erma?" The power of suggestion is overwhelming. To get my mind off where I am, the technician offers to pipe in a radio show. He says it will distract me and make me feel better.

As I lie wedged in my electronic coffin, I hear the voice of a talk show host interviewing Beverly, a madam who runs a house of prostitution in Denver. It gets my attention. Beverly makes more money in a day than I have made in my lifetime. I am so depressed I want to scream.

In keeping with the new laws, physicians are bound to disclose the side effects of the drugs they prescribe. The rule of thumb is that you will never get well with a medicine that smells good, tastes good, and is covered by your insurance.

Modern medicine has a way of complicating the simplest malady. No one has a common cold anymore. It's a virus and no one has a cure for it. They only know there's a lot of it going around.

The first medicine prescribed for me said if I had a heart disease, forget it. If I had diabetes, don't even think of taking it, and if I suffered from hypertension, get rid of it. In other words, I had to be healthy before I could take anything.

The nose drops that I bought carried a warning saying they caused drowsiness and I couldn't drive to work, which meant I could let my nose run or lose my job.

The pill that was to control my fever caused constipation, but the one that was supposed to relieve my congestion might bring on diarrhea. (I figured if I took them in tandem, they would sorta cancel each other out.)

The syrup to stop coughing said I couldn't use heavy machinery. (I interpreted that as the sweeper.)

A liquid to help me sleep could make me nauseous and give me occasional chills. (I already had them.)

The vitamin supplement carried a warning, "Could cause genital itching." I certainly want a refill on that one.

Hanging on to my cold seemed like my best shot.

People usually survive their illnesses, but the paperwork eventually does them in. Filing a claim for insurance is terminal. It sometimes goes on long after you have left the earth. Months after my father died, he not only kept receiving bills from blood labs and the hospital, he was offered a MasterCard with unlimited spending and an invitation to join the Marines.

The cold, hard truth is, no humans staff these offices that process the forms. That is why no one answers the phone. It is all computerized. Once the computer determines you still owe $12.42, you will be dogged for it the rest of your life whether you have paid it or not.

Every day of your life you will sit down at the kitchen table, fill out forms that you have filled out a million times, go to the drugstore and run off three copies of each, and stop at the post office to mail them.

If you should happen to call the insurance company with a question, you must press 1. If you want to hear muzak featuring Barbra Streisand singing "Happy Days Are Here Again" and a recorded voice telling you, "Your call is important. Please stay on the line," press 2. Press 3 if you're frustrated and want to declare yourself incompetent.

The white-tailed deer may be close to a medical breakthrough in treating himself, but ironically, the animal that is most like humans and used in considerable research is the mouse. (Being genetically related to a furry rodent with beady eyes, no waistline, and a tail also depresses me.)

I have never been in a laboratory where mice are involved in research. So when someone tells me they are being used to test the effects of cigarette smoke and alcohol and the consequences of too much sun, I have to believe there's a group of mice sitting around the pool smoking and drinking Mai Tais and working on a tan.

When I hear that jogging mice who get up an accelerated heart rate about three times a week live longer, I get a mental picture of their little bodies being fitted in warm-up suits with the smallest Nikes in the world on their four little feet while they listen to Willard Scott wish them happy birthday.

Recently I read that they milked mice to test the effects of new genetic combinations on protein levels in milk. Forget the results. I want to see the milking stool they use.

What I have a problem with is that if mice have tested every bad habit and disease known to man, from cigarettes, alcohol, drugs, and excess cholesterol to loss of sleep, overbreeding, and bad air . . . then how come there are more mice out there than people?

Every day someone somewhere comes up with an alternative to modern-day medicine. No matter how they try to reform health care, it keeps getting more and more complicated.

I'd like to offer the Robin Leach Get Well or Die Happy plan. Here's how it works. You don't feel well, so instead of waiting for a hospital bed, you check into a great hotel in Los Angeles at a cost of $150 a day. (The hospital room will run you $500.) For this you get a suite with your own television set and a bathroom to yourself. The room comes with a continental breakfast and a newspaper. It also comes with a fluffy bathrobe that covers the ENTIRE body.

There is valet parking for people who come to visit. There are deck chairs and a swimming pool, and when you don't eat everything on your plate, no one cares. You can read until you fall asleep and no one wakes you out of a sound slumber to take your vital signs and give you a sleeping pill.

If you want to elevate your heart rate, you can walk to Rodeo Drive and read price tags. Or if you are bored, you can sit in the lobby and watch people argue over their hotel bill.

If you have a burning desire to see a doctor, there is a putting green nearby where you can meet and maybe have something cold to drink while you tell him what *Reader's Digest* says about your condition.

The biggest plus is that there are no forms to fill out for the rest of your life. Not convinced? What if I told you that for the price of a ride in an ambulance, you could fly first class aboard British Air to London?

There now. I bet you feel better already.

7

*Many animals tend to store things. The bowerbirds
of Australia and New Guinea decorate their
courting grounds with everything from beetle
wings to pilfered car keys. They will hoard
anything. After mating, the male splits and
the female raises the brood by herself.*

*L*est you confuse me with some amateur collector, I
must tell you there are levels of savers. There's the
common garden variety who hoard rubber bands like
they're never going to see another one. And the bread tie
disciples who don't have a clue what they can use them
for, and of course the proverbial plastic margarine con-
tainer freaks who use them to store leftovers they are
going to throw away in three days. They're novices.

No, I'm talking about a woman who still has her
report cards from the third grade . . . food coupons that
have expired . . . single earrings . . . boots with a hole in

one of them . . . and a wildlife calendar from 1987 because February shows a bear in a party hat.

For some strange reason, I have never been able to throw away a cookie sheet. It may look like a drip pan for a 1938 Chrysler and a new one costs $2.95, but, I rationalize, it doesn't have a hole in it.

I never throw away a key. I know that as soon as I do, I'll discover a piece of locked luggage which will be useless because the key is gone.

My husband cannot understand why I have a drawer full of eyeglasses I can't see out of anymore. "They're good yet," I told him. "For what," he retorted, "bumping into walls?"

The madness never stops. It seems every year there is something to feed my compulsion. Take shoulder pads. Please. A few years ago, designers thought they could create an optical illusion. If they gave women shoulders like running backs, their waists would look smaller.

They were wrong. Not only did they give women a Frankenstein silhouette, the pads "traveled." I never got over the shock of seeing four mounds dotting my chest (two that moved). I was going crazy with pads. One day I pulled on a coat with shoulder pads over a jacket with shoulder pads that covered a blouse with another set of shoulder pads. The pads shifted and slipped down my back, causing my friend to observe, "Quasimodo lives."

I take out every shoulder pad I own and am up to my roots in them. They're too big for earrings. Too small for a bleacher pillow. Too light for a badminton shuttlecock. What do I use them for? Eye shades when I want to sleep late? Knee pads for scrubbing the bathroom? Earmuffs? Mitts to polish the car? Potholders?

A friend of mine didn't have the solution but warned, "Hang on to them." (I should point out she's the woman who makes planters out of bleach bottles and Christmas ornaments out of laxative foil.)

What I have is a sickness inherited from my mother. She was a child of the Depression. One of my earliest memories of her was hearing her say to my aunt, "You aren't going to throw those radish tops away, are you?"

Today, she has two cars in her garage, owns her own home, and wears thirty-five credit cards next to her body. She puts on her lipstick by dipping a toothpick into the tube, scooping out a speck of gloss, and transferring it to her fingers and eventually her lips.

When I asked her why, she said, "They don't make Persimmon Jungle anymore."

The family calls her the Box Queen. For as long as I can remember, she has stood at an elbow while a package is being unwrapped. When the contents are held up, the box never touches the floor.

Mother has it squirreled away in a closet somewhere.

Throughout the years, she has become the mecca of cardboard—a one-woman recycling center.

If you are giving anyone a hard-to-wrap chainsaw, she has the box for it. If you have an oversize Elvis painting on velvet, she can put it under wrap for you. Nothing is too big or too small for her to match up with a box.

Christmas, however, is her finest hour.

We learned early that Christmas packages were never what they appeared to be. A small jewelry box with the promise of a drop-dead diamond held a fishing fly.

Mother tolerates Christmas, but what really brings a smile to her lips is the class of boxes that are distributed.

One year we added a new relative to the family who put a Tiffany box under the tree. Mother could barely contain herself. We were to see that Tiffany box every Christmas for the next ten years. Once it held a bird feeder, another time a smoke alarm, and last year, a beach towel.

I was reluctant to admit I was turning into a box junkie when my daughter pointed it out to me at her birthday celebration last June.

I found myself in a tug of war with my mother over a Nordstrom box. She said it was hers originally, and I said she had never stepped foot in Nordstrom's in her life and it was mine. She said she had traded me two Sears boxes for it and I had just forgotten about it.

At that moment, my daughter intervened and asked if we would mind postponing this argument until she opened the contents of the box.

She said I needed help, but believe me when I tell you that I am nowhere near the fanatic about saving boxes that my mother is. Her closets and storage spaces hold nothing but boxes inside of boxes.

I'm not that far gone.

I was ironing one afternoon when Mom dropped by. "What are you doing?" she asked.

"I'm ironing old tissue paper and used ribbons. See? They're like new."

She looked at me and smiled. "This is the first thing you have ever done that has made me happy."

My husband says he doesn't see how much longer this planet can support my hoarding. That is unfair. All of it is not mine. It belongs to our grown children who moved to apartments the size of picnic tables and don't have room for their childhoods.

My guest room, in addition to a bed and a chest, holds six chairs. Are you the least bit curious why my guest room looks like a bus station waiting room? We also have a grill and lawn furniture in the utility room, skis in the storage shed, and a car in the driveway that no one would steal because it has no motor.

It's all part of my mother's laws that I learned at her knee. If it doesn't show, replace it. If you're too full to eat it, save it and throw it away later. If it's too dirty to wash, store it. If it makes you happy when you see it again, put it in the kitchen drawer. If you can't get to it . . . use a toothpick.

8

The cheetah is the fastest mammal on land. A predator, he has been clocked at seventy to seventy-five miles per hour when chasing his objective. He has been known to reach forty-five miles per hour in two seconds.

Compared to the IRS when they cash your check, the cheetah is standing still.

I figure there are one hundred million Americans who file tax returns every year. They are obliged to do so by a certain day or they will regret it for the rest of their lives. Most citizens wait until the last minute. That should mean it is physically impossible for your check to get to your bank in fifteen minutes. The IRS can do it.

The government can't run a postal system that can compete with the Pony Express. It can't run a defense department without buying a plane that is useless and obsolete before it is built. It buys $180 toilet seats and a telescope with a flaw in it, and it hasn't balanced its budget in decades. But the IRS, the jewel in the government's crown, is there for you. It's there when you win a pot at Vegas or a new car on *Wheel of Fortune.* One misstep and you'll be doing time, followed by community service.

By March, every citizen receives a form. It has been written by the same people who write instructions on how to man a space flight.

Do not expect the IRS to have a sense of humor. You've never seen a sitcom on them and you won't. Once I attached a memo that read: "Hey, Bunkie, have you ever had one of those days where you wrote the bank a check for being overdrawn? Your teenager called a 900 number to hear someone talk sexy and ran up a $600 phone bill? Your kid's teeth are growing in like your husband's side? How about an extension?"

The answer that arrived on the same day I wrote the note read, "How would you like to clean toilets at the stadium for every day you miss?"

The refund check is a different story. Speed is no longer in their interest.

You know who else is faster than a speeding bullet? The kid at the car wash. When he drives your car onto the belt, he looks like someone who would nod off during a traffic light. However, during the forty-one seconds it takes your car to travel through the chamois and suds jungle, he springs into action like a predator who hasn't eaten in three days.

By the time your car has emerged from the conveyer belt, he has:

Directed your three mirrors skyward.

Changed the position of the car seat.

Adjusted your window vents to an open position.

Started your windshield wipers.

Turned on your directional signals.

Changed your radio dial to a German-language station that plays twenty-four hours of polkas.

This speed is maintained for only forty-one seconds. He reverts to his normal mode and takes twenty-five minutes to wipe the water off your windows.

It's hard to imagine that a waitress belongs on the fastest-animals-in-the-world list. If you set fire to yourself to get her attention, she'd bark, "More water at table four" and disappear.

I have often wished someone would be honest about it. If they would come to the table and say, "Look, Roxie's sister got sick and your waitress won't be back for two weeks," I could handle that.

Her accelerated speeds occur when you join your best friend for a long, leisurely, catching-up lunch that you've been looking forward to for weeks.

She appears at the table, drops a menu in our laps, and asks, "Want anything from the bar? Would you like to order now? The soup of the day is minestrone." She stands there tapping her pencil on the pad.

We both order drinks and lunch when my friend says, "You're gonna die when I tell you this."

The drinks and our lunches appear before the sentence is finished. "More coffee?" she asks and drops the check onto the table.

"Order more coffee," I say. "I'm going to the restroom."

When I return, she is replacing the tablecloth. The entire lunch took eight minutes. Had we chewed our food, it would have topped at ten.

Another entry that may surprise you is doctors.

A visit to your physician's office is not unlike preparing for a big vacation trip. You start early to shower every part of your body, use body lotion and powder, put on clean or new underwear, and make plans to arrive just a little early.

You sit in a waiting room with a half dozen patients and play the wonder-what-he-has game. You read the diplomas on the wall and try to figure out the doctor's age. You read a 1983 *People* magazine and realize everyone who was married is now divorced. You are down to a magazine called *Colon Newsletter* when you are called. You have been sitting there for seventy-five minutes.

You enter the examination room and sit on a cold table. Another fifteen minutes have passed. The nurse pokes her head in the door and does the warm-up. "The doctor is on his way."

More minutes pass before the doctor arrives.

He says, "How have you been feeling?"

You say, "Okay."

He says, "Are you still on . . ." and proceeds to name all your medication. You say yes.

He says, "Great, see you in a month."

Total time, twenty-three seconds. I've had longer visits with the guy at a toll station.

Sometimes it seems like the world is on fast-forward. We can't wait for nails to dry, or food to cook. We have to know the sex of the baby as soon as it's conceived.

The more I think about it, the more there is to be said for the sloth. He sleeps fifteen to eighteen hours a day and is known to have taken forty-eight days to travel four miles. He hangs in the trees after he's dead.

But he lives longer than the cheetah.

9

Male lions confine themselves to an area varying from 15 to 150 square miles in which other lions are not tolerated. Males patrol their domains—leaving calling cards of scent mixed with urine on bushes and tufts of grass. This discourages any other animal from entering their territory.

There are two things you notice when you enter an aerobics class for the first time. First, no one needs to be there. String thongs divide small hardened buttocks, leotards span flat, firm stomachs, little white arms dangle like Virginia Slims.

The second thing you notice is that everyone but you has a "spot." There are no lines drawn, no reserved spaces, and no permits issued, but somehow everyone marches to her mat and is ready to defend it to her death.

Actually, the idea of joining an aerobics class never

entered my mind until one night when we were sitting around the living room watching the Olympics. My son said, "Hey Mom, you've got legs like Dan Jansen." I looked at the speed skater as he sped around the track, his body doubled over like a collapsible tray table, and saw his spandex thighs. They could have supported a bridge. "I can fix that," I said. "My muscles just need a little toning."

If the aerobics class had been a ship, it would have sunk before "Nearer My God to Thee" was played. Everyone in the class was jammed in the last two rows. I saw one mat left and put my body on it. Everyone stopped talking.

"What?" I asked.

"You're in Helen's spot."

"Who's Helen?"

"She'll be here. And she won't be happy if you're on her mat."

"How do you know it's Helen's mat?"

"Passion."

"Passion?"

"Elizabeth Taylor's Passion. Mine is scented with Opium, Jan's is Eternity, and Barb's is Nina Ricci."

"Then I'll move up a row."

"That mat belongs to Pat. It's subtle, but it's a bubble gum scent."

While I was wandering around looking for a place to hide, Helen appeared. I hated her. She had hair long enough to pull back and secure with a clasp. She didn't wear underwear under her tights, and she had a chiffon scarf around her neck that she tied around her waist. Her tights bagged at the knees. I had owned bigger pets than Helen.

I ended up in the last place I wanted to be: the front row. At close mirror range, cellulite magnifies.

For three months I was delegated to the front row until one day Nancy (second row, Tiffany) moved to St. Louis. Soon after that, Mabel (third row, excessive sweat) got a job and transferred to a later class.

One day in the dressing room, Barb whispered, "Don't tell anyone I told you, but a back row spot may be opening up soon."

"Who?"

"Doris [Coriendré] may have back surgery. When she returns you'll have to challenge her, but it's a great spot."

"Where is it?"

"Back row, right by the door and the drinking fountain."

"That's prime."

"I know."

A few weeks ago a newcomer to aerobics put her towel down on my mat.

I smiled. "You are in my spot."

"I didn't know you could own them," she said.

"You are wrong."

"So what if I don't want to move?"

"Does the term 'a seal in mating season' have any meaning for you?"

She picked up her towel and headed for the first row. She will learn as we all had to do that that's the way it is in aerobics class. You get your spot and your parking space in front of the building the old-fashioned way—you fight for them. There are few who leave the class and have their mats reach hall-of-fame status. One is Sandra Day O'Connor, with whom I used to do aerobics. When she left to take a position in Washington as a Supreme Court justice, they retired her mat.

My mat was retired three years later. They made a parking lot out of it.

My family thought this was amusing, but I pointed out, we are all territorial about something.

We sit in the same pew at church and have our "spot" in the family car. Even Archie Bunker had his chair.

Global wars are fought over territory, so it's not unusual to have a marriage threatened when you stake out which side of the bed you are going to sleep on for as long as you are wed.

It's one of the rare times when mixed marriages work. A wall person should never marry another wall person. However, if you are a wall sleeper and you choose a close-to-the-bathroom mate, success is within your grasp.

On our honeymoon, I said, "I'll take the outside of the bed."

"Is that important to you?" he said.

"Yes. I have kidneys the size of lentils."

"What's a lentil?"

"A small grain you make soup out of. Is this a problem for you?"

"Yes. I get up a lot."

"What for?"

"I recheck the door to make sure it's locked. I check the car to make sure I turned off the lights. I make sure the toilet isn't running. I check to make sure I didn't leave the key in the front door when I came in. I cough a lot, and I go in the bathroom and shut the door to do it so I don't wake everyone up."

"Maybe you should give up your day job," I said dryly.

"Maybe we should just cut off your liquids at 6 P.M."

In getting the outside of the bed, I had won my first big battle. I had dibs on the bathroom and control of the bedside light. When I was sleepy, the lights went out. I felt I had triumphed until the birth of our first child. The experience turned out to be a shallow victory. The baby was born nocturnal. When there was a cry in the night, I was closer to the bassinet, so I hauled out. In the morning I would say, "Why didn't you take care of the baby?" He answered, "I didn't hear it." It's remarkable what a difference seven inches and all the covers pulled over your head can make.

One day I returned home to find his car parked in my spot in the garage. This is something you have to call when it happens or it can get out of hand.

I marched into the kitchen and announced, "You are parked in *my* spot."

"*Your* spot! How did it get to be your spot?"

"The minute you gave me that clunker for a second car that leaks more oil than they lost in the Persian Gulf. That grease spot is mine, so move it!"

10

*On June 17, 1987, the last remaining dusky
sparrow died in Titusville, Florida. He was the last
of his species. Since 1600, 109 species of birds and
many additional subspecies have disappeared from
the earth.*

I remember them in numbers too great to count.

They swarmed about you from the moment you
entered their territory to the moment you moved on. At
times they were pesky and you wanted to spray them
with something, but the upside is they were there when
you needed them.

Everyone thought the American salesperson would
last forever. She knew where the other sizes were buried,
the assortment of colors in the back room. She would
special order for you, process returns, and discreetly open
the dressing room door half an inch and slide another
garment inside.

Then salespersons turned into the hunted and shoppers became the predators. To find one was nothing short of bagging a trophy.

We would wander up and down the aisles staring at breasts in search of a name tag. I once went up to a young man and asked, "Are you in bras?" and he said indignantly, "I beg your pardon."

As their numbers decreased, their security increased. They would put you in a dressing room and lock the door. I had a recurring nightmare that someday they would forget I was behind the door, everyone would go home, and I would be sentenced to twelve hours of staring at my cellulite.

What brought about the extinction of the salesperson? Technology. A microchip could talk to us on elevators, and machines could serve us beverages and sandwiches. We could paw through the merchandise ourselves, and if someone was tempted to take it without paying for it, you could have an ugly piece of plastic that set off an alarm and dangle from the hemline for the rest of your life. We began stripping in public. We were talking to ourselves.

Salespersons weren't the only ones to disappear from the workforce. Human bank tellers were replaced by drive-up machines that spewed out money as you stood there. We could pump our own gas and check out our own library books. Factory workers diminished.

We have a son who once was fired from three jobs in one day. In the first one he didn't feel comfortable telling people that van Gogh sometimes painted on velvet and this was an original for $49.59. He was a valet who parked cars for a Hollywood party and lost the keys to one of the cars. The third job, he was a waiter in a Mexican restaurant and asked a table of eight, "Could I get you anything else, sir?" and the man answered, "Yeah, the menu."

We gave him the American dream speech.

"You get a nice steady job. Doesn't matter if you hate it, just so it's steady. Then you work at it twenty-five years and at the end of that time they give you a watch and give your job to a summer replacement."

He informed us that wasn't the way things worked anymore. There were no "steady" jobs. The old standards were being phased out: newspaper reporters, specialist physicians, Wall Street lawyers, and mathematicians.

If Dustin Hoffman were pulled aside on his graduation day and given one word for success, it wouldn't be "plastics," it would be "funeral director." I know it doesn't translate to a cute license plate, but that is the hottest job going now.

According to government projections, the number of deaths will reach 2.4 million in 2005 and 3.1 million in 2025.

I pulled my son aside and said, "Pizza delivery. Americans will always be too lazy to go for their own pizza. Trust me on this."

We're getting so crazy. I dialed my best friend the other day, put down the phone to turn off something on the stove, and when I returned started to tell her about a woman who ordered thousands of dollars in catalog stuff so she could see her FedEx man, when I realized I had been talking to her answering machine for twenty minutes.

Every day in our society another of the human species ends up on the endangered list. But it's the salesperson I miss the most. One day there will be a monument to her, with a plastic ID covering her chest, sturdy shoes, and keys to the showcase around her waist. A small plaque will identify her and contain four little words that will ring unfamiliar to most gazers: "May I help you?"

11

---

*AT&T has signed up the animal kingdom.
Every creature that can be darted and sedated for
five minutes wears a beeper collar to record
his whereabouts. A Swainson's thrush has a tiny
radio embedded in his neck so he can be tracked.
Even monarch butterflies wear tags to trace their
travels. Animals can run, swim, or fly . . .
but they cannot hide.*

I hear a buzzing sound. Is it the cellular phone? The portable phone? The fax? The pager? The timer on my oven telling me my brownies are done?

One cannot live in the twentieth century and not be accessible at any time of the day or night. It's reminiscent of calling my kids. After they had run up from the basement of a friend's house where they were playing, jumped over two fences, dodged traffic, raced through a sprinkler, and breathlessly appeared at the back door and asked, "What do you want?" I answered, "Nothing. I just wanted to know where you were."

You want to know how crazy all this communication has become? A woman in Idaho needed to call her daughter, so she switched off her TV to mute and dialed her number. Nothing. She was annoyed. She knew her daughter was home. Why was she not answering her phone? As she was dialing again, she noted her TV set going nuts. "Now," she thought, "I need a TV repairman to boot." She slammed down the instrument and was hit with the realization that she couldn't get her daughter on the phone because she had been dialing the number on the remote control.

For a long time my husband and I resisted an answering machine. It was a big step for two people who still use carbon paper and a typewriter with Wite-Out droppings on the keys.

When he brought the box home, we looked at it with the same apprehension cavemen must have felt when they saw fire for the first time. We inched in slowly for a closer look, not daring to touch the buttons, afraid of what they would do.

"We have to record a message," he said quietly.

I froze. I had heard other people's messages and they all were cute, funny, and original. Why was it that everyone who wasn't at home was at the Comedy Store doing his act?

I had heard, "Hello there. I'm out social climbing, but if you leave your name and number and if you're anybody, I'll get back to you."

There was another friend who intimidated every caller with, "Leave a message. If you don't, you'll regret it for the rest of your life. Maybe not today or tomorrow, but if I were you I'd take my phone off the hook."

One day I got a wrong number of a person doing Mister Rogers. "Mr. Whirley is not home right now but please call back. Remember, you'll have to use Mr. Tongue and Mr. Lips."

Every time I called one of my sons and he wasn't home, I prepared to grow old. He laced his voice with helium and his message said, "You have reached the law offices of Bernstein, Weinstein, Bombeck, and Springsteen. If you have a personal injury, press 1. If you are suing, press 2. If you need help quickly, press 3." By the time I sat through all of that I forgot what I called for in the first place.

"You bought the machine," I told my husband. "You record the message. I want no part of it. Say what you want. I'm out of it."

He grabbed a piece of paper and scribbled, "We're not home now . . ."

"They know that," I interrupted. "If the callers have any sense at all, the moment it rings and no one answers, they'll know that. You're just wasting tape."

"I thought you wanted nothing to do with this?" he questioned.

"I don't. It's your machine. You call the shots. I'm history."

"We are unable to come to the phone," he continued writing, "because we are out or away from our desks."

"It's none of their business," I said. "I suppose you're going to tell them when we're in the bathroom or watching the last three minutes of a game."

He started again. "You have reached Erma and Bill. If you will just leave your name and number at the sound of the beep, we'll get back to you."

"Speak for yourself," I said. "There are some people I don't want to talk to."

"Then don't call them back."

"After you just told them I would?"

The first night the machine was in operation, we were having dinner when the phone rang. "Don't bother to answer it," said my husband. "I have the machine on."

We sat there in silence through six rings before it stopped.

"This is great," I said. "No more interrupted meals. No more running like a crazy person to pick up before they hang up. This is wonderful."

"I told you. We should have gotten the machine a long time ago."

We ate in silence.

"Who do you think it was?" I asked. "Everyone knows we eat at six."

"Could be long distance," he said.

"Could be the police asking us to identify someone," I said.

We left our hot food and raced together to push the play button. It was a woman inquiring if we wanted to renew the warranty on our microwave oven.

"You're the one who said you'd call back," I growled and returned to the table.

If we can't be reached by phone, the fax can. It is fast replacing the human voice. At a singles bar, the question is no longer, "Hi, I'm Bambi, what's your sign?" It's "What's you fax number?"

At a high school reunion, a former Miss Montana was holding court with her classmates by telling them she had wanted another baby to fill the empty nest and her husband didn't.

When asked how she pulled it off, she smiled slyly and said, "It was easy. When we replaced the bidet in the bathroom and installed a fax machine, he was home all the time."

We were hesitant about adding another piece of technology to our home (which is decorated in early business machines) until we read that during the Jewish holidays more than ten thousand heaven-bound messages were faxed to the Wailing Wall in Jerusalem. They ranged from asking help in the lottery to "I'm Lutheran, but I'm covering all bases."

I figured if God had a fax it had to be a good thing.

The first fax I sent was to columnist Art Buchwald, who had been ragging me about living in the twelfth century. It was clever. It read, "Mr. Buchwald, come here. I need you. Alexander Graham Bombeck."

Upon receiving no response, we called his secretary, who told us to turn our machine on. Nothing. The paper jammed. We tried again. After twelve phone calls, we received a letter by express mail from Art, who said, "You are not fax material. It's nothing to be ashamed of. Shakespeare never had a fax machine." He said he'd try again in a month when we had the hang of it.

A month later we heard beeps and belches, but no message. Art called and said he didn't want to spend another $930 to send a message. He said, "Do you have to put quarters in your machine or what?"

I told him to try again.

He called on the phone and said, "You're pathetic. What would happen if Ed McMahon tried to fax that you had won the American Family Sweepstakes?"

I told him Ed McMahon never faxes. He comes to your house in person with a check and a camera crew.

"So while you're on the phone, why don't you just tell me the message."

He said, "The message is, 'If you receive this fax, send me six signed bookplates for your new book. If you do not receive this, we are buying six copies of Geraldo Rivera's new book instead.'"

Beepers, on the other hand, are the designer jewelry of the nineties. I've worn one for three years and gotten three pages: two phone numbers of drug dealers and one telling me my batteries needed replacing.

I don't know who we think is going to call us on all these devices, who cannot wait. Is Robert Redford going to say he'll be late for dinner? Will the president need to get our advice on the health bill?

It's only a matter of time before we read about the first beeper transplant in humans. We'll see how it works out with the Swainson's thrush.

12

Animal behaviorists concur that the least intelligent animal walking the face of the earth (especially on the fourth Thursday of November) is the turkey. He will freeze to death when there is warmth nearby and has to be persuaded to eat when he is starving.

Another animal who is three races away from a triple crown is the agouti, a South American rodent. When observed by researchers, he dug up a sweet potato and did three things:

He peeled the sweet potato.
He ate the potato.
He ate the peelings.

Homo sapiens have to be in the top five who live life with their dimmers on.

In the seventies, my friend founded an organization

for the Incredibly Stupid and Dumb Beyond Belief. There were no meetings or dues, but there was a trophy she had picked up at a garage sale. It was a small nude statue of a man in a loincloth with a club in his hand. The statue was a revolving award that went to whomever had the guts to admit to screwing up.

It has had many owners. One was a friend who left his lens cap on his camera while filming fifteen rolls on his vacation. My husband had it at one time for leaving his passport on top of a hotel TV set in London and having to pay an empty cab $40 to pick it up and rush it to the airport.

I can't remember the reason he sent it back East, but the statue broke in transit, and he got the award back for being stupid enough to send it in a shoebox wrapped in newspaper in the first place.

My mother got it when she paid $3,000 for a battery-driven wheelchair for my father to tool around the house, only to discover it wouldn't fit through the door frames. We didn't actually give her the award until she sold the chair for $1,000. That corked it.

Pouring boiling water from a spaghetti pot down my stomach didn't make me stupid enough for the award. Telling my mother about it did.

The human race are masters of the ridiculous. There was actually a story in our newspaper of a man who was bitten on the tongue while kissing a rattlesnake. He decided to try a nonscientific remedy he heard about to counteract a snakebite. So he wired his mouth to a pickup truck battery and tried to jump-start his tongue.

It knocked him out cold and he ended up in the hospital, where he lost part of his tongue and one lip.

In another story, KLM Royal Dutch Airlines made an offer the world could refuse. For $80 you could board one of their planes and go wherever it happened to be going and ride it back again without ever getting off. Their PR man was obviously overmedicated.

Crooks are the worst of all. We can't build jails fast enough to keep pace with all the men and women who "had a plan." There's the guy who robbed a convenience store and as he was escaping realized he needed a get-away car. He picked the one nearest the street . . . a police car with an officer at the wheel.

Another guy was ripping off a little old lady. He tied her up and had all her furniture stacked near the door to cart off. Then he noticed some pills by her bedside and figured they were speed. He gulped them down. They were tranquilizers. He fell asleep before he could leave and was awakened by the police.

If anyone knew where they were, I'd send the ISDBB award to the two guys who tried to break *in* to the Ohio penitentiary. When the guards sent up warning shots, they fired back. They wanted in and were scaling the wall with a rope. Guards finally drove them away. What did they think it was? A cotillion to which they hadn't been invited?

The lifetime achievement ISDBB has to go to the robber who got stuck in a pawnshop chimney for two days in temperatures that dipped into the twenties before police found him.

He would not say what he was doing there, but it's my guess he shouldn't have missed his Weight Watchers meeting.

Automation is not helping matters. Children born to computers have the jump on those of us who struggle but are still computer-dead, software-challenged, and sit frozen at the wheel at the thought of merging on the information highway.

I remember when the first nonhuman tram came into existence in the Atlanta airport. The train came to a stop, the doors opened automatically, and seventy-five people formed a funnel to get inside the door before it crushed them to death.

Once I was inside, the muffled recording of a voice that sounded like it had just come out of surgery told me to step away from the door and wait for my stop. I was terrified that I would spend the rest of my life trapped in a tram in Atlanta.

As I was returning from a trip to California, I dropped by an airport rest room.

In my stall, I wrestled with my jumpsuit to keep it from falling on the floor. As I was doing so, the belt fell into the commode. Before I could retrieve it, the automatic flusher sucked it away and into the sewers of San Jose.

I put myself together and at the washbowl stuck my hands under an automatic water tap. As I went for the paper towel in a machine on the wall, I turned in time to see my handbag fall into the sink and activate the water once more. It proceeded to drown.

I will eventually die at the hands of automation. I don't know when or where, but it will happen. An automatic elevator door will squeeze the life out of me. An automatic seat belt will glide across my chest and cut off the air to my windpipe. A talking scale will destroy my self-esteem and send me to an institution.

Although a plethora of humans are lucky to get through each day, there are a number of animals who aren't swift. Take skunks. They are killed on the highways by motorists in great numbers. Instead of running away at the approach of an auto, they stand their ground and use their biggest defense: spraying.

I've had the Incredibly Stupid and Dumb Beyond Belief award since last Thanksgiving. Here I was dealing with a turkey, the dumbest member of the animal kingdom, and when I called everyone for dinner, the bird still looked pale. It seems I had cooked it using the price instead of the poundage.

13

The Central Park Zoo in New York paid an animal behaviorist $25,000 to treat a polar bear named Gus for boredom. Although his condition didn't interfere with the animal's eating, sleeping, or sex drive, Gus just swam all day in the same repetitive pattern. To alleviate his stress and add excitement to his day, therapists gave him a beach ball covered with peanut butter to lick.

Comfort food has long been a treatment for boredom for the woman who is home alone. It isn't until her rear end begins to look like a Woodstock parking lot that she realizes licking peanut butter off a beach ball is not the answer to her problem.

Within the last decade, there has been an alternative to food to help women escape boredom: TV. Not your ordinary game shows and *I Love Lucy* reruns, but talk shows.

They're like junk food for the mind. They contain no

calories and no nutritional value whatsoever. But they seem to satisfy a need.

There are nearly fifty talk shows currently on the air. On a given day you can listen to the stories of bisexuals who fell in love with the boy *and* the girl next door, transvestites who complain they can't buy coats with sleeves long enough to cover their arms, and women who have *not* had sex with their pool men.

This has clearly become the decade of the dysfunctional. Grandmothers who hit on their granddaughters' boyfriends . . . Polish gymnasts with eating disorders . . . and married couples who both engage in prostitution because the pay is good and they can sleep late.

For years, talk shows featured celebrities who talked about their careers and their last movies.

The public wanted more.

Lately, the pre-interview with superstars goes something like this.

"So, what's happening in your life?"

"I just finished a movie."

"That's great. Tell me, were you ever molested by your mother or father as a child?"

"No, I don't think so . . ."

"They never burned you with a cigarette and put you in a closet?"

"Gosh no."

"Make my week! Tell me you've been to the Betty Ford clinic."

"No."

"Your kids writing a kiss-and-tell book on you?"

"Uh-uh."

"You're making it hard for me. You don't have some fatal disease we could milk, do you?"

"Not that I know of."

"A yeast infection . . . anything! Anyone suing you—leaving you penniless?"

"No."

"I got it. Your spouse is leaving you for a sixteen-year-old."

"No."

"Look," says the talent coordinator, "I gotta be honest with you. If we put you on the air with that kind of background, the audience would be asleep in five minutes. When you have something disgusting to talk about, have your people call my people."

The attraction to these shows isn't too hard to figure. You may have been fired from your job, had your husband walk out on you, lost your health plan, and had your twenty-six-year-old divorced daughter move back home with her two children, but at least you're not as bad off as the woman on *Oprah* whose husband was sleeping with her sister and her mother, and all three of them were carrying his baby.

It's a mystery to me where they find all these problematic people and why they are willing to go on television to talk about it. The hosts all say, "It'll make you feel better to get it out in the open." *Oprah* says it. So do Phil and Sally and Geraldo; Jenny, Montel, Maury, Vicki, Ricki, and all the others. My concern is how big is the supply of dysfunctional people. Are we nearing the bottom yet? Or is the day close at hand when we'll be glued to our sets watching Maury Povich wring a confession out of a girl who got a pimple on prom night and how she handled it.

If *Homo sapiens* ever discover a common language with animals, however, talk shows will open up a rich vein of bizarre behavior from the wild kingdom.

OPRAH: "Today you're going to meet and hear one of the most bizarre stories of violent sex since Lorena Bobbitt. Meet the sea otter. (Applause, applause) Tell us a little about your courtship."

OTTER: "Well, you couldn't exactly call it a courtship. This male I had never seen before in my life grabbed me from behind and clamped his jaw on my head, neck, nose, and upper jaw. My nose was nearly severed. He held me under water most of the time so that I thought I was going to drown. I could hardly breathe." (*Starts to cry*)

OPRAH: "We feel your pain. How long did all this brutality last?"

OTTER: "It lasted about twenty minutes and he was gone."

OPRAH: "So, he impregnated you and took off."

OTTER: "They always do."

OPRAH: "You became a single mother. How did you feel about that?"

OTTER: "Pretty good, actually. This clown wasn't exactly a day at the beach. I don't care if I ever see him again. But the worst part is that I'm scarred for life. (*Close-up of otter's raw nose*)

OPRAH: "Are you self-conscious about that?"

OTTER: "Well sure, everywhere I show my face people look at me and chant, 'We know what you've been doing.'"

OPRAH (*staring into camera*): "There's more. We'll be right back after this commercial break."

SALLY JESSY RAPHAËL: "For all of you in our audience today who think birds and some other animals mate for life, hang on to your hats. We have a panel who doesn't know the meaning of the word 'monogamous.' I think it's proper to call this panel 'serial sex offenders.' First, we have the barn swallow, who has a fooling-around rate of forty percent."

BARN SWALLOW: "Thank you."

SALLY: "We have a lion—how shall I say this?—who isn't

really particular—and has been known to mate eighty-six times in one day. Is that right?"

LION: "I wasn't counting."

SALLY: "Next is the red-sided garter snake, who has been known to join a hundred or so of his buddies to mate with a single female."

SNAKE: "That is correct."

SALLY (*taking off glasses*): "You're a transvestite, aren't you?"

SNAKE: "It happens."

SALLY (*smiling*): "What these animals will do for sex, you're not going to believe. This is the male crab spider. Tell our audience about your encounter with a female."

SPIDER: "Well, to begin with, the female is a lot bigger than we are and as soon as we approach her, she begins to chew our heads off."

SALLY: "You're joking."

SPIDER: "No, she really starts to chew our heads off."

SALLY: "But then how . . ."

SPIDER: "She leaves the rest of the body to sexually function so that the sperm can continue to pass through."

SALLY: "Is there any way you can fend off these attacks?"

SPIDER: "Some males pack a lunch, so to speak. We bring food to distract her—you know, keep her busy. . ."

SALLY: "Did you know she was frigid?"

SPIDER: "Yes, but it's worth the challenge."

SALLY (*tears in her eyes*): "Let me give you a hug."

PHIL: "You're looking today at deadbeat parents—guys and gals who said 'I do' and did, but took off. I call your attention to the bull elephant seal—four tons of sea stud who impregnates as many as forty females in one fell swoop, then goes for a long swim.

"And if you think he's a sweetheart, take a look at the sea turtle, who hits the beach, digs a hole, drops her eggs, and is history.

"Call me a cynic, but I don't think the salmon is going to get too many Mother's Day cards. Listen to this. She lays eight thousand eggs in a stream . . . then splits to let them hatch on their own. Eight thousand of them. I gotta ask, don't you ever feel a little bit of guilt for abandoning eight thousand of your kids?"

SALMON: "I think it makes them more self-reliant. Too much mothering can ruin a child."

Phil: "Hold your questions; we'll be right back."

Today it sounds ridiculous. But don't count out hearing a Geraldo teaser some day, "Do gorillas dish the dirt? A Stanford University primatologist says so. Join Koko, Liz Smith, and Cindy Adams—on the next Geraldo."

14

The blue whale is the largest inhabitant of the earth. He weighs eighty tons and is one hundred feet long. His tongue is bigger than an auto.

We all have 'em. Those days when we feel like we're retaining more water than a rain forest. You know you're sensitive about it. Especially when two people stand up on a bus and offer you their seats. You want to slap Jenny Craig.

If you get a dress to fit your hips, you have enough material left over from the hem and sleeves to slipcover Brazil.

Your car fits snug and you wonder if bloat is life-threatening. To make your day you pick up a newspaper and read that Sylvester Stallone appeared in a film in the buff and was quoted as saying, "I must admit that I performed well. It was a good nude day."

Give me a break! Do I need to hear that? What is a good nude day? Have I ever had one?

The only thing worse than not having a good nude day is having one and not knowing you're having it.

I'm willing to bet good money that not too many people have them. Models for Rubens and Michelangelo were obviously having bad nude days when they posed for posterity. Look at them on canvas. They look like they just ate their way into a pasta coma.

If you're ever in the Sistine Chapel, just look up at the ceiling. You can tell at a glance which model had water retention and which one gave up sucking it in.

Frankly, the Statue of Liberty could drop a few pounds. Oh sure, she's tall—151 feet—and disguises her size by wearing a caftan, but she weighs forty-five thousand pounds. According to insurance charts, she should top off at about thirty-five thousand pounds. It's not easy. How many of us have said, "I'm going to lose that extra ten thousand pounds by Christmas"?

I've always considered myself a loser when the new body part trends are announced. If bosoms are high this year, mine have succumbed to gravity. If the waist is going to be "important to fashion," I can't find mine. If large eyes are important, mine stopped growing when I was ten.

You cannot imagine my excitement a few years ago when I read that fat rear ends were back. I had never had a body part that was "in" before.

The fashion industry was actually touting—and I'm quoting directly from Paris—"The derriere is in fashion focus as designers play up the bottom with added fabric, lace, and even a bustle."

For the first time I felt sorry for those flat-bottomed girls who walked themselves to death on Stairmasters to nowhere. I wanted to pull them aside and say, "Look, honey, you don't need to kill yourself developing fanny muscles. I've grown my own rear end and it's no big deal. How do I do it? I drive to the mailbox, bank from my car, drop off and pick up my cleaning from the car, and drive for hours to get a spot just outside the door of my aerobics class.

"I use my children as slaves. They find my glasses, run errands, get me a drink of water, let the dog out, and answer the door.

"At night I sit in a chair with all the amenities around me: popcorn, soft drink, and TV tuner. That way I don't have to move for five hours.

"In a matter of months when you walk across the floor and your legs rub together, you will swear you are being followed by a group."

Unfortunately, the trend also applies to men. The more rounded the behind, the more women are turned on. This is sad because most men have rears that look like someone let the air out of a whoopee cushion. They can't sit on a wicker chair without causing themselves great pain. They have to work on it.

But with women, all they have to do is sit and wait for their bottoms to spread.

Most women will not believe it is this easy and will opt for fat transplants. For the record, I'm a universal donor.

Just when I was beginning to feel good about myself, scientists came out with a full-force attack on overweight people to "shape up." They said Americans spend $33 billion a year to lose weight and still are blimped out.

That is because people don't know dieters at all. They are conniving, clever, sneaky people who will try every diversion they can to keep from cutting back.

They will become pregnant just to wear comfortable underwear.

They will pour gravy over seven-grain bread.

They will eat a Quarter Pounder, a basket of fries, a serving of onion rings, and a piece of fresh cherry pie and put artificial sweetener in their coffee.

No one wants to face the reality that he eats too much and exercises too little.

My sister had a dog named Wendy. She was a Pomeranian who looked like a ball of black yarn. Wendy was fat and spoiled. If she wanted to go from the living room to the kitchen, my sister carried her. If all the chairs were occupied and the only one left was the big overstuffed one occupied by Wendy, the dog held firm. You could lean against the wall for two hours and she wouldn't move. Every night there was a bedtime ritual. She would be placed on the countertop in the kitchen and await a large bowl of ice cream.

In time, Wendy was so fat, her bark sounded like a slow leak in a tire. My sister took her to the vet, who said she had to lose weight or she wouldn't be around much longer. My sister found a small dietary can of dog food that cost $2.29 and stocked cases of them.

I said, "Couldn't you just feed her less food?"

My sister looked at me and said, "You've never liked animals."

That's the mentality of dieters. They want to believe you can buy your way to thinness.

If you took a poll of the entire population, ninety-nine percent would say they are not happy with their bodies. If you admitted to being happy, no one would speak to you. Supermodels who walk and nothing moves groan and say, "I'd like to lose some of these thighs." It makes them seem more like "one of the girls."

Like most women, I read all I can about dieting. I want to believe I will live longer if I eat healthy and exercise on a regular basis. But one thing troubles me. Whales live on a diet of fish (no meats or pastries) and they exercise twenty-four hours a day. They couldn't buy a dress off a rack if they had to.

15

A Chesapeake Labrador dog named Curly traveled 650 miles from Billings, Montana, to Alexander, North Dakota, between December 1 and December 23. After arriving in Alexander, Curly slept for seventy-two hours, then decided to leave and went back to Billings.

I was never caught up in the jogging/running movement that swept the country in the seventies and eighties. Face it, I call a cab to go to the mailbox.

It is not reasonable to run 26 miles and 385 yards to stand in line for a cot to pass out on. If I wanted bloody feet, I'd buy size $4^1/2$ heels.

I am married to a man who had a TV tuner transplant so he wouldn't have to look for it all the time. You cannot imagine my surprise when he decided to run marathons.

But what really threw me for a loop was that he saved

himself for the races. He could run over twenty-six miles in three hours and thirty-three minutes. When I called to him, "Dinner!" it took him thirty-five minutes to cover a distance of eighteen feet. Go figure.

I don't know what men do to kill all that time. The call to come eat automatically triggered something in my grandfather that would send him to the bathroom, where he not only used the facilities, but afterward rearranged the medicine chest before appearing at the table. By that time the steam was off the potatoes and the smile was gone from Grandma's lips.

For the last two decades, people did dumb things in the name of recreation. They weren't games like tennis or Ping-Pong in which you kept score and someone won or lost. They were stupid things young people did that prompted younger brothers or sisters to ask before they embarked on their adventure, "Can I have your record albums if you don't come back?"

One of these sports was bungee jumping. A bungee cord was attached to a bridge or a tower and people simply put the loop around their waists and jumped off. If they didn't smash their brains out, they did it again. Sometimes they paid as much as $80 for the thrill.

I remember the first time I saw a rock climber. He weighed about thirty-eight pounds and for no reason was scaling a mountain of rock that looked like a wall.

I have known fear before—like having my bowling ball bounce into the next lane, or knocking my tennis ball into the clubhouse dining room, or being the only person to ride a chairlift round trip at the ski slope because I couldn't ski off—but rock climbing! What would happen if you thought you were grabbing one of those little bolts and it turned out to be a snake's head? What if you got halfway up and your shoe came untied?

The incredible part of rock climbing is that it is a sport that isn't criticized for its danger, but is attracting the attention of environmentalists who say enthusiasts are causing damage to the planet.

How many people are we talking about here who go out on a Sunday and dig their fingernails into solid rock? Ten? Twenty? Thirty, tops?

Call me when there is rock gridlock.

I don't run and I don't climb rocks, but I did succumb to another dumb recreation that made its debut in the early nineties: stair climbing.

I told my husband I was joining a health spa and for three days a week I was going to go to a gym, turn on a machine, and climb stairs.

"Remember that two-story house we lived in in Bellbrook? You used to stack laundry at the bottom of the stairs and make one trip a year."

"I don't remember that," I said.

"You said if God had meant for you to ascend to the second floor, He would have awarded you frequent-flyer mileage."

"I never said that."

"There were diapers in that pile the day the last kid graduated from high school."

"Are you finished?"

"No. Remember that trip we took to Ireland? You

were going to kiss the Blarney Stone until you saw all those steps."

"When you're married to someone for forty-some years, who needs to kiss another stone?" I said.

I didn't care what he thought. I bought a cute little stair-climbing outfit and went to the gym for about three weeks before I decided my rear end still made flapping noises when I walked.

Children are born looking for something meaningless that causes their mothers to speed up the aging process.

One of the sports that sent me into premature menopause was skateboarding. It wasn't enough for my son to plant his feet firmly on this little piece of wood with rollers on it and sail through the mall scaring people half to death. He discovered an arena built like a teacup in which he skated around until his body was parallel to the other side, and he came as close to the top as he could before flying into the parking lot. When it began to snow, the skateboard was replaced by a snowboard.

Rollerblades became insurance companies' worst nightmare as thousands of kids tried to balance themselves on skates that went at out-of-control speeds.

No one knows for sure why Curly traveled thirteen hundred miles when he didn't know anyone to visit and there wasn't a sale. I'm guessing he did it for the same reason two men climb on a luge with no brakes, lie on their backs with their upper bodies protruding over the sleigh, and steer blindly down a tunnel of ice at speeds of seventy to ninety miles per hour. Because it's something to do.

16

*The hippopotamus is a vegetarian who weighs two
tons. His lips are nearly two feet wide.*

The human female animal has never been happy with
the way she looks. It's just been within the last decade
that she has done something about it. She has done a lot
about it.

Who could have predicted that in the nineties, hippo
lips would become sexy? Film stars Barbara Hershey and
Faye Dunaway had theirs enhanced and looked like they
whipped through a drive-in cosmetic surgery station,
rolled down the windows, and commanded, "Check the
pressure on my lips and pump in a few pounds of colla-
gen."

It left them with the same sneer on their faces that
prompts mothers to say to their children, "Get that look
off your face, missy, or you're going to spend puberty
chained to your bed!"

Women of the nineties should be carrying signs around their necks that read, "Remodeling in progress" or "Pardon our dust. We're under construction." In the pursuit of youth, they are having the fat sucked out of their thighs and arms, bags removed from under their eyes, chins lifted, tucks in their tummies, and breast reductions or augmentations (depending on whether they can see their plates when they look down to eat).

The race for maidenhood has been won by a few. Barbie is thirty-six years old and doesn't have a single spider vein on the back of her knees to show for it.

Dick Clark is sixty-five years old and comes straight from the kingdom of Shangri-la.

Mickey Mouse is sixty-six. I don't know how a rodent is supposed to age, but I'd say an animal on Medicare is a little old for short pants.

What is the obsession about staying young? Growing old is a natural thing. Miss America grows old. Leftovers age. Cars deteriorate. Houses fall apart. But we fight to the death to hang on to the body we had at the prom even if we have to encase ourselves in spandex.

Any day now I expect to see an elderly woman on television cry out to her alarm system, "Help me. I have fallen in my spandex bodysuit and I can't get up."

It is my theory you can't get rid of fat. All you can do is move it around, like furniture.

Take a cupful of thunder thighs and add it to the bosom. Or take a little off your breasts and use it to pump up your buttocks. How much hips do you want in your cheekbones? One lump or two?

I have no intention of bulldozing my fat around, but the other night I sat down and took a blank sheet of paper and drew a line down the middle of it. One heading read "Fat In" and the other read "Fat Out."

I looked at my stomach and figured I could lose a couple of quarts and put it under "Fat Out." Then I looked at my thighs and ankles and figured I could shed a pint or so and not miss it. That also went under "Fat Out." No doubt about the fat glut under my arms. It went in the "Out" column.

To make a long story short, when I tallied up the "Fat In" column, it came out zero. When I added up the "Fat Out" column, I had enough for another person.

We are certainly not the only animal that grooms itself. Animals in the wild are obsessed with grooming. Chimpanzees pick at one another constantly. Otters spend the biggest part of their day maintaining their beautiful fur. Some birds engage in "anting." They flop atop an anthill and let the angry residents swarm over them. One explanation of why they do this is that the ants' formic acid clings to them and discourages parasites. Another theory is that, given the bird's dazed look, the acid may be an addictive substance. (Remember, these are professionals. Do not try this in your home.)

Humans get their highs in other ways. Those who don't wish to opt for expensive surgery have been uplifted by the Wonder Bra. It lifts and separates in a way you never dreamed was possible. (The wonder of it is that there is only one person inside it.) The waist nipper is a popular item that gives you a smaller waist but makes your hair taller. And there is, of course, the Butt-Booster that picks your sagging derriere off the floor and gives it form.

In the mid-nineties a strange phenomenon occurred. Men who acted like they didn't care about their bodies developed an awareness. Most of them had come from an era in which, if they could see their belt above their waist, they had it all under control. When their belt dropped a couple of feet and could have substituted for a truss, the flab had taken over. So what?

The cover of *Psychology Today* featured a man, Lucky Vanous, who was a construction worker in a Coke ad. Every day at 11:30 he took off his shirt to have a Coke. His audience was a group of swooning office workers who planned their break around him just to see his sweating muscles. According to the magazine, he represented a major social change. Men are now the objects of desire as women have been.

They discovered they could market their sensuality. It opened up a new road for men. They appeared in style shows, ads for cologne, dance groups that performed for women only (happy birthday, Peg Bundy) and strippers' gigs at bachelorette parties for women with liberal friends and a new mother-in-law who couldn't see too well. It also triggered a downside: eating disorders, constant dieting and exercise, and an obsession with how you look or how much cosmetic surgery you can afford.

Beefcakes are falling into the trap. There are ads for rear end enhancements, and pumping iron has become a national pastime. It is only a matter of time before these male sex gods will join the rest of us females in the hourly quest for youth. I'm a woman who is so cheap I refuse to call a plumber. I reseat the toilet with Play-Doh. However, when it comes to getting rid of my eye wrinkles, I will let my health insurance policy lapse rather than give up my rejuvenating cream. I cannot walk down a cosmetic aisle in a store without stopping to check out the magic elixirs, creams, and sealers.

I really believe that a white cream under my eyes will make the bags disappear when bellhops refuse to carry them. There is no doubt in my mind that I can have Katharine Hepburn cheekbones in a Shelley Winters body.

The other day a skin specialist suggested I needed a "repair kit."

"Are we talking extra parts here?"

"No, no," she said. "We're looking at a cell breakdown. Just a few dabs a day and the crevasses around your eyes would disappear and perhaps we could do something about those laugh lines."

"I haven't laughed in fifteen years."

I bought the facial repair kit. I put it in the trunk of my car with the tire jack, flares, and spare tire. You never know if you are going to be out alone on a dark road some night when your lips go flat!

17

Squirrels bury nuts haphazardly—five nuts every three and a half minutes until they have more than ten thousand stored. Contrary to myth, they only remember where they hid half of them, and the nuts grow into trees.

The mind is a very selective thing.

I remember every person who ever borrowed a book, a sweater, a pen, a plastic leftover dish, or money and has not returned it.

I remember my grandmother's phone number from 1939, the verse and chorus to the "Beer Barrel Polka," the Gettysburg Address, and the identities of the entire cast of the Mouseketeers.

I cannot put the right name to my kids the first time around. I stare at them and stumble through the names of the first two and end with, "You know who you are. Answer the phone."

For mothers, the memory game starts early. We begin by hiding things from the little ones. Not just laundry bleach and drain cleaner. We stash birthday cards, Christmas bicycles, Scotch tape, pencils, the key's to Daddy's workroom, chewing gum, and the television tuner.

But mostly, like the squirrels, we hide food. I have put cookies behind the water heater, candy in a laxative box, bananas in the guest closet, and taco chips under the dish towel (the last thing they'd pick up).

We never remember where we put it.

When I was growing up, I had the mind of a computer. I could tell you the exact day and hour my sister got her first watch and when she was allowed to stay out beyond midnight.

Later in my life I forgot little things—like where I left the kids and when to pay our insurance premiums so they wouldn't lapse—but that is because I was on overload.

As I got older my memory didn't matter. I didn't have anything worth remembering anyway. I just chased teenagers and shopped for over-the-counter sedatives.

It was when the kids left home that my husband and I began to notice our inability to recall people's names and places. It drove us nuts.

We couldn't remember the names of all the dwarfs in *Snow White* or identify all the Kennedys. (We always left out Eunice.) And we knew if one of us started a sentence, the other one had better be in the room to fill in the gaps.

I love to tell my "back" story, but I need my husband to tell me what the procedure that gave me relief is called. It just slides off his tongue—automated percutaneous lumbar discectomy. If I notice he isn't in the room, I substitute my "calcium in my shoulder" story. It's not as dramatic, but calcium I can remember.

My husband can never remember Phil Jackson's name (coach of the Chicago Bulls). So when he gets to the end of his story he clicks his fingers at me and says, "What's his name, Erma? The guy who looks like Tom Selleck with a migraine?" And like a trained seal I bark, "Phil Jackson."

One night I had to go to the bathroom and as I heard him telling the story, I leaned down and whispered in his ear, "Phil Jackson" before I left the room. He thanked me.

Both of us like to watch *Jeopardy!* just to keep our minds sharp and alert. One night I sat up in bed and shouted in the darkness, "What is *Peyton Place*!" My husband came out of a sound sleep and said, "What are you talking about?" "Remember when *Jeopardy!* asked for the book by Grace Metalious that shocked New England?"

"Alex Trebek asked that four days ago," he said.

"You can't hurry genius," I said.

Our kids think our deterioration is amusing. They point out with some regularity that we are losing one hundred thousand brain cells a year.

You cannot imagine my exhilaration when I read in a reputable magazine that brain cells may shrink, but they don't necessarily die.

Thank God something on me is shrinking!

The story said when they put old rats (were they wearing Depends?) in cages with new toys, their brains exploded in activity and the blood flow to the brain was increased. This effect diminished after the novelty wore off and they became bored.

You don't have to knock me over with a two-by-four to convince me that the secret of youth is never getting bored. According to the findings, watching *Jeopardy!* or sports does not stimulate the brain. Neither does running. However, crossword puzzles and walking will keep your brain young and alive. Go figure.

The statistic that grabbed me was that the mind is not the first thing to go. Come to think about it, I have noticed a slow, but gradual breakdown.

In my twenties, I got glasses. This happened soon after I went to a restaurant and before I ordered dropped the menu on the floor and before picking it up said, "I'll have the spinach tortellini and the house salad." Everyone else at the table held the menu in their hands.

As I settled into my thirties, my knees and feet began sending messages. My tennis serve slowed down to a pace where if I jumped the net, I could have returned it to myself. I noticed that when I entered a social event, the first thing I looked for was a chair.

The back and the kidneys started in my forties. Every one of my contemporaries had the same problem. The women talked openly of their nocturnal path to the bathroom, and as with everything else that was falling, blamed it on childbirth.

My mind went sometime in the fifties. I couldn't find

my car in the mall, couldn't recall if I added salt to the potatoes, and not only couldn't remember the punch line to a joke, I couldn't remember the joke.

Sex is up there in the first five things to quit on you. Where it is on the list depends on how serious the other four are.

The article made me think that I should make some changes in my life. I resolved to start working crossword puzzles at least once a week, walk every other day, and get me a toy—possibly Harrison Ford.

18

In Saudi Arabia, a motorist accidentally killed a monkey on a highway in the Khamis Messeit region. Later, while driving home on the same road, he found monkeys still gathered around the dead animal's body. The mourners spotted his car, jumped on it, and smashed his windows.

Animals seem to handle death better than humans. Whether they retaliate or walk away from it, closure is swift.

Humans, on the other hand, ask why, conduct a viewing and an elaborate ceremony, bring in trays of cold cuts and potato salad, and send the deceased to the cemetery in the first limo he's been in in his life.

Grief is not instinctive in our species. It must be taught. Children rarely have a clue what is going on. In northern California, a woman lost her pet and felt bound to explain the life/death cycle to her five-year-old daughter. She drew the child close to her and whispered, "We can all be happy now that Frisky is up in heaven with God."

Her daughter looked at her without emotion and asked, "Mom! What's God going to do with a dead dog?"

Since our children mothered every animal they could trap in a Mason jar, we attended a pet funeral nearly every week of our lives. There was a small lizard who lived in a terrarium on the back of the commode, whom I suspected died of "flush anxiety." We put to rest a pet beetle; had there been an autopsy, it would have revealed half of my hall carpet. There was a memorial service for a hamster who opted for the death penalty by biting our electric toaster wire in half.

But the most poignant of the services were the ones we conducted for deceased guppies at the toilet bowl, or what we affectionately called the Heavenly Aquarium.

We'd all stand around the rim staring into the water and I'd ask if the guppy had a name. (They always did.) Then I would ask each child to say something appropriate and nice about the fish. Sentiments come to mind like, "She didn't smell until last night." "She didn't bite anyone." "I'm sorry I fed you pizza, Ethel."

We all agreed Ethel had had a good life and one of the kids would unwrap her body from a nose tissue and drop it into the toilet. We commended her body to the plumbing and flushed. I told them Captain Ty-D-Bol would guide her personally to that big sewer in the sky.

I am not saying all wild animals are without feelings

or do not grieve. I have seen film of elephants who have lingered over their dead for hours, trying desperately to pick them up with their tusks and trunks to force them on their feet again. When you can't take a pulse, that's what you do.

A common trait shared by both humans and wild animals is our determination to survive. People prolong death with parts and replacements. There are even legal decisions to be made by humans on how long they want to live.

Some animals have the enviable capacity to heal themselves. A lizard regenerates his severed tail, starfish and crabs can regrow their limbs, and sea cucumbers can even jump-start their intestines into growing back.

Being cute will give an animal a longer life expectancy than he deserves. Find a scorpion on your wall and bam! he's history. Get a Yorkshire terrier and he hangs on for two hundred years.

We owned a Yorkie whom we could not train. When people would ask my address, I would say, "The kennel at the top of the hill. Call first."

He barked, he bit, and he wouldn't use the doggie door unless you held it for him. We shopped for a new owner who would give him a wonderful home. The potential owner said, "Isn't he adorable? Does he bark?" We said yes. "Wonderful," she said, "that will keep burglars away. Does he bite?"

"Yes," we said lamely, thinking she'd give him back.

"Perfect. That will discourage people from coming around the house."

As we turned to walk away, leaving him in his new home, he jumped up on her Edwardian satin-covered couch, dropped a bomb, and snuggled in the cushions.

"He is so cute," she gushed.

I knew he would outlive her.

There is an unwritten law that the more demands a pet makes on you, the longer he will live.

I once owned a parrot who spoke only two phrases, "Hello Barney" (the fool was saying hello to himself) and "Telephone." I was attracted to the pet because he was a lot like my husband. He'd tell you his name and when the phone rang would shout "Telephone!" but make no move to answer it.

Barney's ritual was the same every day. He ate a pound of grain and went to the bathroom enough to overflow a landfill.

His life span was estimated at one hundred years.

One day I was in a pet shop and saw a speech training cassette.

As I stood in front of Barney's cage dangling the cassette in front of him, I said, "Look, big fella, for three years you have done nothing but dribble peanut shells all over the floor and occasionally fly over my typewriter and make tapioca. Is it asking too much to have you communicate? I'm not asking you to line dance—only say something."

The instructions were simple. For twenty minutes twice a day the bird would listen to two repetitive phrases, a soliloquy from *Hamlet,* and arias from *Carmen* and *Madama Butterfly.*

The phrases were "Hey, I'm over here" and "I'm a bad bird."

Then he was supposed to tra-la-la along to twenty minutes of the "Toreador" song.

By the end of three weeks I was considering making a necklace of Valium and licking it at intervals. The cassette was driving me nuts.

With the kind of care he was getting, he'd outlive me. The kids made it plain they did not want to be left anything they had to dust, finish, or feed. With Barney's limited skills he couldn't make a living. I would have to provide for him in the will.

One evening at the dinner table my husband said, "I'm a bad bird." Then he added, "I have no idea why I said that."

I know why he said it. It was the stupid cassette. Since I had one of them talking, I made a present of Barney to my son who loves animals and who has a better chance of outliving him than I do.

I've watched a sea turtle give birth on the beaches of Costa Rica. There is a tear that rolls down her cheeks as she delivers. Some say it's just a tear gland and has nothing to do with the pain of giving birth.

I like to believe it's because she knows she will never see them again.

19

One of the most watchable animals in the wild kingdom is the gorilla. He will belch, hoot, bark, cry, roar, do somersaults, slide down a hill on his stomach, spin on a rope, or examine private parts of his body in detail to gain attention.

all it a wild theory of mine, but I think exhibitionists are born that way. He's the baby in his crib who cries like he has just swallowed a razor blade, and when you pick him up he stops.

He's the child who, in every home movie, sails across the screen in front of everyone like a blurred Frisbee out of control. At the dinner table, he will dangle a French fry from each nostril and bark like a seal. He wets in the wading pool, clearing it out in fifteen seconds. He wears his clothes inside out to school and lets his underwear hang out of his tennis shorts. For show-and-tell he takes your checkbook to class. When he grows up he frequents karaoke bars and sings "Strangers in the Night"—off-key.

The majority of *Homo sapiens* live quiet lives in the bleacher seats. They are content to sit back and watch the attention seekers.

This leaves a select group who carry cards in their billfolds reading, "In case of accident—call a press conference."

So how does one go about getting attention? In the animal kingdom a male millipede will bang his head on the ground at the rate of five times a second. That gets a crowd.

Or if you want to make a human statement, you could be like the artist who, along with two hundred volunteers, created a two-mile-long sand sculpture of twenty-one thousand size 34C breasts on a beach in California. His next project is to string ten thousand bras across a mile-wide stretch of the Grand Canyon.

But humans have an attention getter that animals in the wild don't have—nudity. Madonna bared herself from the waist up at an AIDS benefit. The only thing we haven't seen of Madonna's is her X rays.

Howard Stern, the New York talkmeister, appeared nude on the cover of his book, *Private Parts*. He outsold authors with their clothes on ten to one.

Roseanne has been known to moon a group of bystanders, sing the national anthem off-key with her hand in her crotch, and announce to the press she is going to have a ménage à trois with her former husband

and a secretary—and that was just one Sunday morning.

They are professional exhibitionists and most of these things should not be done in your own home. But there's a big chunk of the population who will fulfill Andy Warhol's prediction that everyone will have celebritydom for fifteen minutes.

Heading the list are the lottery winners. Here's a couple sitting around the house doing nothing when they hear their numbers announced on TV. Within minutes, their front yard is overflowing with photographers and cameramen and bloodsucking relatives from as far away as Hawaii. Helicopters circle. Just before hyperventilating, they say into the camera, "Oh my God." Asked if all this money will change their lives, they say, "Absolutely not."

I will never forget the story of the lottery winner from Ohio who won $50 million. When asked what he was going to do with all that money, he was quoted as saying, "I've always wanted one of them eight-slice toasters."

Is that the American dream or what!

Of all the luxuries that torment people but elude them, a toaster doesn't seem to be one of them, but what do I know? Maybe there are dreamers who lie in a hammock, stare at the sky, and plan for the day when they can make toast for an entire Marine base.

The irony is that most lottery winners lust after some small thing that probably has been within their grasp all along. So they wish for something they've been putting off . . . a new sofa for Mama, a trip to the Smokies with the kids, or as the man from Ohio added, "Fill in the dents in my Pinto."

Another recipient in New York State's lottery retired early to a modest house to "order take-out food and save for when we're poor again."

Ridiculous, you say? How long have you had a cookie sheet that looks like a bad patch of road? You could probably pick one up for $2.95, but instead, you open the window to get rid of the smoke each time you use it.

I've fantasized about winning the lottery and being a celebrity on all the newscasts. I've always wanted an extra set of door keys. My husband's dream is a set of salt and pepper shakers for the table so he won't have to walk to the stove every meal. Hey, as long as you're dreaming, why not reach for the stars?

The instant celebrity I like to watch is the one on the six o'clock news who has lived next door to a serial ax murderer for six years and didn't know it. The camera catches him as he's standing on the curb watching his neighbor being taken away. A TV reporter sticks a microphone in his face and says, "This is Elwood Merk who lives next door to the suspect. Did you notice anything unusual about him?"

Mr. Merk, realizing he's on camera, smiles and says, "Gosh no. He seemed like a real nice fella. Walked his dog every night, very quiet. Even bought a box of cookies from my daughter. She's a Girl Scout. I believe they were chocolate mint, weren't they, Evie?" His wife nods.

Television does have a way of bringing out emotions people have hidden for years. Classic examples are the

114

new shout-degrade-and-humiliate talk shows that have surfaced for the younger crowd.

The perks are that you are brought to New York, delivered to a free hotel room by a limousine, made up by a professional makeup artist, and then released into an arena of strangers who will hear your story of divorce, infidelity, kinkiness, or bad relationships. And here's the entertainment part: You must sit there while the audience calls you "slut," "tramp," or worse and reduces you to tears and beyond therapy.

It's a terrific price to pay for fifteen minutes on TV and a little blush and eyeliner.

Was it only a few years ago that Bob Eubanks asked a couple on *The Newlywed Game* which way they were facing when they made whoopee? "Was it the Arctic Circle, South America, or Ohio?" The audience gasped. Was there ever a time when we had a game show called *I've Got a Secret?*

There are no secrets anymore. All you have to do to get your fifteen minutes of celebritydom is use your imagination. A guy on the David Letterman show flexed his pectoral muscles to "Dueling Banjos" for two minutes. "The audience seemed to like the act," he said, "but then any time you disrobe in public, it gets applause."

It's hard to believe that there is still a segment of the population that can resist the notoriety. They simply want to be left alone.

The animal kingdom is emphatic about it. When someone approaches the hognose snake, he doesn't want a confrontation. He simply turns on his back and lies with his mouth open and his tongue limply out. If he is touched, he remains perfectly rigid and appears to be dead. The predator usually goes away.

This is not unlike husbands who do not want to be bothered during a Super Bowl game.

The sea cucumber gets even a little more drastic. He prefers to spend his life where he was born, and when anyone or anything approaches him, sends out a message by ejecting all his innards before he collapses.

Think of the ratings you could get on that!

20

Dogs and cats can earn free bonus flights under Carnival Air Lines' new frequent-flyer program for pets. They must ride in the cargo hold, are not served free drinks, and must be accompanied by their owners. (In the cargo?)

Everybody loves a bargain.

Now cheap is downright chic. If I had been told that someone as shallow as me would be caught up in garage sales, secondhand shops, factory outlets, and Loehmann's look-alikes, I wouldn't have believed it.

However, I have a gift. I can drive on a godforsaken patch of highway with nothing in sight but concrete and trees, sniff the air, and announce, "I smell an everything-must-go sale."

I have a radar system. My hair stands up like an antenna and my feet take me right to a stack of bedsheet seconds. Although I haven't balanced a checkbook in more than thirty years, I can compute percentages in less time than it takes to say, "Charge it."

Shopping is like everything else in this country that became more aggressive and violent in the nineties. The women in white gloves who regarded browsing through the department stores as a pleasant outing turned into a group of pit bulls with attitudes.

We pay a price for this aggressiveness. We suffer the humiliation of communal dressing rooms surrounded by women wearing only knee-highs and a handbag.

We dress in the aisles so we won't have to give up our spots at the sale table. We walk around with red raw necks where a ripped-out designer label reminds us of our sacrifice.

I have been known to travel an hour by plane to a consignment shop that advertises clothes formerly owned by movie stars. I paid 75 cents for a vest Debra Paget supposedly wore in a Western. No one cared.

If a jacket has a lipstick stain on the collar and a label by Donna Karan, we don't care. If the skirt won't meet and has to be tied around our hips with a rope and is made by Bill Blass, we'll spring for it.

If a sweater has a small moth hole and was designed by Mondi, we'll slap a name tag over it.

We emerge from our shopping battles like warriors, clutching our raggy little trophies which we have fought for so desperately.

Just when it seemed like the malls and factory outlets couldn't get any bigger, along came PriceCostco, supermarket planets covering acres of land and stocked with floor-to-ceiling bulk merchandise.

It is not a place for those who cannot commit.

The shopping carts are larger than our first apartments. To keep out the nonserious shoppers, the store requires a membership.

I filled out my application, paid my $30, and posed for my picture. "Is there a dining room?" I asked.

The girl behind the desk stared at me, then handed me a coupon for a free hot dog and a beverage.

"I don't suppose there are golf privileges." I laughed nervously. She remained silent.

I turned around to survey my newfound playground.

Everything I had been taught about buying only what I need and eradicating waste had to be rethought. I had to imagine that I was a frontier wife coming into town in the buckboard once a year for supplies . . . a cook who had five thousand Marines to feed on bivouac . . . a missionary who was en route to a Third World country and would be upriver without supplies for three years.

I began to buy. If the country ever stages another Woodstock for two hundred thousand people with weak kidneys, I have the toilet tissue for it. If anyone wants to stuff a mattress with trail mix to make it firm, look no farther than my pantry. I have dental floss that will outlast my teeth. In short, I went nuts.

I bought a can of tomato paste I couldn't even lift. Cat food that will last for the next twenty years went into my cart—longer if I don't get a cat. I purchased a wedge of cheese that looked like a wagon wheel. The good news is that bulk shopping prolongs your life. Who's going to die with twenty batteries for smoke alarms and two drums of oatmeal?

I bought a copy of my own book—because it was discounted.

I bought a carton of bagel dogs. I ate them in one week.

Don't ever mention the name bagel dog to me again.

There's a strangeness about being held captive in a store where you are surrounded by foods that are bigger than you are. They seem to dominate you. You wonder if anyone else feels the same way. I found myself going up to perfect strangers and saying, "Would you like to share fifty pounds of lettuce?" Some were grateful for the offer and said, "Only if you split a dozen bottles of laxatives with me."

We vowed to meet in the parking lot.

There's something spiritual about saving money through bulk shopping. In many ways we feel superior. Especially after the loading-the-car experience. Most cars are not equipped to transport all that food. Only sixteen-wheelers with interstate licenses are equipped to transport all that food.

My mother and I loaded the trunk carefully, one item at a time. Then we filled up the backseat and began strapping things to the top of the car. When we finished, she balanced a wheel of Brie between her knees and clutched ten pounds of cold shrimp next to her chest. As I started to drive away, we noticed a fifty-pound box of Miracle-Gro that we hadn't packed on the pavement.

Our only choice was to put wheels on it and tow it home.

Bargains are seductive, whether it's bonus airline miles or coupons from the Sunday paper. Somehow the struggle sets us apart from the home shoppers who watch Diane von Furstenberg tie a scarf fifteen ways and dial the shopping channel to order five of them.

It's like saying you served in the war when you drove the general's kids to baton-twirling classes.

I'm not an armchair shopper. People who talk about an eelskin wallet for twenty minutes or carry on for half an hour on what a charm bracelet with circus horses on it can do for my life leave me cold.

Shopping by TV versus combat is the difference between watching a tennis match and playing Andre Agassi on center court.

I love a bargain and if I have to fly between the hours of 2 and 3 A.M. on a Wednesday during Lent dressed as Newt Gingrich in the months when oysters are in season, I'll get a free pass for my dog on an airline whether he wants to go or not.

21

---

*There is a rare goat with a strange genetic disorder.
When frightened or excited, he will freeze and faint
dead away. I know what you're thinking. Yes, he
still mates without incident. One can only conclude
sex isn't as exciting as it's touted to be.*

A reader once wrote a letter to Ann Landers asking her
advice about what she should do if a married man
had a heart attack while having sex with her in her bed.

Do you have any idea what the odds are of that happening? About the same as Mister Rogers dancing on
the table with Madonna. No one wants to admit it, but
sex in the nineties is boring.

The problem is that it has gone from an active act to
a spectator sport. We watch people make love on television and in films. We call 900 numbers to hear what
someone would do to us if they weren't sitting in a boiler

room of other dirty talkers reading from a prepared script.

We rent tapes of what happens when stewardess Cindy locks the bathroom door of the plane at thirty-four thousand feet.

Sex crimes invade the newspapers and are the main topic of conversation on talk shows.

We leaf through centerfolds and can't wait for Miss July to appear on our calendars.

Nakedness sells everything from bras to beer.

So how come our thirty-year-olds are sitting home Saturday nights with a pizza and a rented film?

With all the precautions and risks that accompany sex today, it sounds about as much fun as walking through a minefield.

I've never seen a generation work so hard at finding the perfect union. There are support groups for those who "can't commit," dating services for prospects who sell themselves via video, and, my personal favorite, the newspaper ads that employ a language known only to other hopefuls. For example, MSF (male seeking female) or FSM (female seeking male) has two lines and four days to sell themselves to a prospective date. They abbreviate their qualifications: NS, no smoking; ND, no drugs; DM, divorced male; DF, divorced female.

I read one ad by a retired military officer who said he sought "attractive stable homebody"—an oxymoron if ever I heard one. Another wanted someone to run outdoors with him and enjoy the quiet country life. So why doesn't he buy a dog?

This indecision has produced a generation of nervous mothers whose only qualification for an in-law is, "Does he have a pulse?" Mothers haven't finished their jobs until they see their children at the altar saying, "I do" to a house they can't afford, a car that won't outlast the payments, and children who will take away their will to live. Only then can they smile, sit back, and get a life.

The patron saint of these mothers is Queen Elizabeth II. The woman has done it all. Marriage in 1947 sounded great to her. All she was obliged to do was keep ten castles going, wave, smile, and give the House of Windsor heirs. She should have heeded the words of Queen Charlotte, wife of King George III. After the birth of her fifteenth and last child when she was age thirty-eight, she gasped, "My quiver is full." (The British do have a way with words.)

It wasn't that easy for the queen of England. You try to marry off three sons to virgins and have a husband who walks two feet behind you, a widowed mother living with you who wears a hat to breakfast, and a daughter who points her finger at an obese guest at Buckingham Palace and shouts, "Is all of that you?"

Every time she got one married, she'd pick up the tabloids to read one of them had split. For the heir to the British throne, Prince Charles, she threw some kind of wedding. (It was rumored the olives alone cost $40,000.)

In front of the world, the prince picked up with a married woman with a bad perm. As for the queen, here is a woman who should be enjoying life with none of the responsibilities of running a monarchy and she ends up having to pay taxes and recycle her sequins.

I doubt if the animal world has these kinds of problems. Oh, some will have exotic mating rituals and display themselves to the female. Others have no finesse whatsoever.

But even they are being exploited as a peep show. There is an annual "sex tour" at the San Francisco Zoo, followed by a champagne breakfast. Hey, if Smokey the Bear is a hunk, I don't care. If a baboon parades around topless, don't call me.

We have done a pretty good job trivializing sex in our own kingdom without dipping into the animal phylum. A few years ago we made a hero out of a lion named Fraser who fathered an astounding number of offspring. Had he not died, the Democratic Party would probably have run him for president.

My husband and I were in Africa, witnessing a mass migration of wildebeest. You could barely make them out for the dust. A misstep from just one would have been disastrous for those coming behind. As I trained my binoculars on the extravaganza, I couldn't believe my eyes as a male wildebeest mounted a female and had a quickie. I turned to my husband and observed, "Animal!"

Just twenty years ago, China gave the United States two pandas, Hsing-Hsing and Ling-Ling. Scientists followed them around like a bad habit, showing them slides and sex manuals, hoping to get a baby panda born in captivity. Well, you try to conceive with CNN focused on you day and night.

Those of us who have climbed over the islands of the

Galápagos are hearing stories of how our intrusion is beginning to reflect in the reproduction of birds. Their rituals are being interrupted and their numbers are at risk. What may be a "Kodak moment" for tourists may well contribute to the birds' extinction.

Humans seem to have fostered a generation who say yes to everything. Just do what you want—whenever you want.

I think a lot about the goat with the genetic disorder. What does excite him enough to make him drop like a stone? If it isn't sex, what is it? Is it food? Does his mate announce, "We're moving"? I know what would make me pass out cold. Someone who would say, "Good Lord, your roots are coming in white."

22

Chimpanzees live thirty-five to forty years. Very aged females seem to show signs of menopause.

*W*hat would those signs be? Does one aging chimp shove another out of the tree for no reason? Does she cry when the last berry on the tree is rotten? Does she wake up in the middle of the night and scream, "I don't know about you, Leroy, but I'm losing the fur coat"?

My mother was always vague about menopause. When I asked her what it meant she said, "Your baby basket dries up."

"Is that the clinical description?" I asked.

"That's what it amounts to."

"Is it something to worry about?"

"Only if you hate dry skin, migraines, itching, palpitations, hot flashes, sweats, depression, apprehension, nervousness, insomnia, and crawling sensations under your skin."

Grandma called it "the change," and both of them never took their eyes off me after I passed the age of forty. Every time I'd say, "Could we open the door in the kitchen and get a little air? The oven has been on all day," they'd give each other the same look as they did when my cousin had a premature baby that weighed eleven pounds.

"Maybe you're going through the you-know-what," said Grandma.

Mother smiled. "You're not too young, you know."

It was as if they couldn't wait for me to be miserable.

Heaven knows I had enough to throw me into an early menopause. I was teaching a teenager to drive who had to look at the floor to find the brake, and my body looked like someone had just pushed the down button.

When the hot flashes first started to come, it was the first time I'd been warm since I got married. My husband's idea of heaven was to throw open the bedroom window each night and see a glacier under it.

We argued constantly, not only about the thermostat in the house (I pioneered cryogenics), but about the temperature of the car.

I didn't see why you couldn't just get in a cold car, push the heat button, and have heat. He explained to me in great detail how the system worked and said it would heat up in twenty minutes. In twenty minutes I would be at my destination, so what's the point?

As the hot flashes progressed, I became the first

human to survive a meltdown and make breakfast the next morning. After a visit to my friendly gynecologist, I said to my mother, "What do you think of hormone replacement therapy?"

"You can get makeup to cover the mustache."

"What mustache?"

"The one you're going to get without the hormones."

"What are my choices?"

"You could go insane like the rest of us."

At age fifty my reproductive function had come to an end. My biological clock was no longer ticking like a time bomb.

The biological clock isn't just a buzz phrase. It exists in humans and it exists in mice. The clock gene in these little rodents has been isolated and found to control time that passes with each activity. Scientists say with more study it could open the door to developing drugs to fight jet lag, help night workers, or treat sleep disorders.

So what could it do for the children born in the sixties who decided to do some last-minute shopping for a baby before their clock was replaced with estrogen supplements?

A lot of their optimism at having a baby in their late thirties is the fault of movies and television. How many films have you seen in which a serviceman picks up a girl at the USO, has a cup of coffee, and nine months later she is meeting his ship at the dock with a baby in her arms?

Many young women wait to give birth until they are fulfilled in their careers, they get the house of their dreams, their marriage is secure enough for them to have stretch marks, or their bad perm grows out.

A woman announces at a board meeting that she is going home and conceive a baby and will be back in exactly ten months. You would think she was ordering a turkey for Thanksgiving.

Thirty-whatevers have discovered it doesn't work that way. A baby is conceived when it wants to be conceived. In vitro fertilization, sperm banks, artificial insemination, and adoption notwithstanding, there are tried and true ways to get pregnant.

Buy a two-seater sports car, go into hock for a home you cannot possibly afford, and diet until you reach your birth weight. It'll happen.

Some of today's women are doing it the hard way . . . without a husband. The whiptail lizard has lived forever without males. They reproduce parthenogenetically and create new individuals by an infertilized egg, without the need for fertilization from males.

I've always been intrigued with the variety of answers this generation will give their children who ask, "Where did I come from, Mommy?"

They will range from "Number 176 vial in Buffalo, New York," to "You were defrosted."

Like most women of my generation, I am curious as to how they will handle menopause. If they're busy having babies, they won't have time for it. If they postpone it, they'll just think it's old age and call a hotline for help.

23

Many animals are migratory and follow the sun. Crows, bobolinks, geese, and ducks travel south in groups. Butterflies that normally lead solitary lives will cluster and head for Florida, Mexico, and the Monterey Peninsula.

Humans throughout the world also have an infatuation with the sun. Nothing will stop them in their pursuit of it—neither three dysfunctional children fighting over two car windows, vibrating beds that won't stop, or $8 hamburgers, of which the child eats the pickle and leaves the rest.

I spent most of my life in Ohio. I had nothing to live for except my two weeks each year in the Florida sun. Women who didn't have a job to go to hibernated in their houses nine months out of the year. They've done studies of the effects of dark days on people, and it's not a pretty sight. We tend to eat continuously and watch ourselves outgrow our maternity underwear. So what! The Florida sun is seven months away.

The inertia causes our heart rates to slow down, we sleep a lot, and we experience shallow breathing.

Some of us go heavily into crafts. Even before Martha Stewart got her first glue gun, I was making Christmas ornaments out of pill bottles, napkin rings out of buttons, and crumb scrapers out of paper plates cut in half.

Only humans tough out the winters in the Midwest. The plants die, the driveway cracks, and the birds all fly south or follow cruise ships.

But there are only five more months to go until Florida.

Little things become a source of irritation and you cry a lot. When my yeast expires, I grieve. I read junk mail and subscribe to the only magazine I don't have: *Truck Pull Personalities*. Every day I etch out "HELP" on the frost of every window in the house.

Filling in the time is challenging. I alphabetize my meat in the freezer, call time-of-day just to hear a human voice, and get the dog a hysterectomy.

Only three months until I see the sun.

I really get creative with cooking, celebrating every day on the calendar. On the anniversary of the *Titanic*, I made meatballs shaped like icebergs. I made every recipe on the Bisquick box—in one day. I visited my thin clothes in the attic.

Then one day, dark clouds moved away and a pitiful

ray of sun struggled to show itself.

Spring had come. It was time to go to Florida.

I move into gear like an old pro. First, there are new underwear and bathing suits to buy. (As if someone five states away would point and say, "That little girl wore the same blue-and-white floral print suit last year.") Then there are cover-ups that are worn over the suits to keep the sun off their bodies.

Everyone has a different tolerance, so there are varying numbers of sunblock to be purchased, plus dark glasses to protect their eyes from the light. Each sun worshipper has to have a beach hat to keep the sun off heads and faces.

Given the age of our car, the low parental level of tolerance for pain, and the bladder muscle control of the three kids in the backseat, the trip takes about three full days.

As we cruise through Fort Lauderdale, cries go up to "Turn on the air. We're dying here." As the sun increases, visors flap down and shirts are hung from the windows to keep the rays out.

We pay $180 a night for a room that has a big seashell for a washbowl and a sandy carpet. The first thing we do is to pull the draperies to keep the sun out.

After we unpack, everyone gets into suit, cover-up, hat, dark glasses, and beach towel and bastes with sunblock.

We had waited nearly a year for this moment, and my last words to the kids are, "Don't get too much sun or you'll get sick!"

Since ocean water magnifies the sun's rays, I opt for a

plastic chaise longue next to the pool ... covered from head to foot and looking like I've just fallen out of a sarcophagus. I shade my eyes and tip an attendant to move my chair into the shade.

We repeat this exercise for the next two weeks.

One of the few animals who has more frequent-flyer miles than most of the Midwesterners in search of the sun each season is the Arctic tern. Each year of their lives they fly from the Arctic to the Antarctic. They see more sunshine in a year than any creature on earth. They rack up twenty-two thousand miles a year. If they travel with young terns, it may only seem that long.

24

In Spain, the Barcelona Zoo is adding a new animal species to its collection: urban man.

Urban man will live in a fenced area, and during visiting hours the public will be able to observe his actions. He will be fed by a zookeeper. Unlike his caged neighbors, a group of chimpanzees, the human will wear clothes and not perform his "private necessities" in public view.

It is rare when *Homo sapiens* roam on wild animal turf. They like to think they're doing it when they go to Africa. They buy a $200 safari jacket and live in the bush in a tent. But having a shower before being served a five-course dinner on a white tablecloth isn't exactly a test in survival.

Most people think of Dian Fossey as a human who

crossed over when she frolicked in the grass and made grunting noises with a group of silverback gorillas in Rwanda.

But generally, humans are not exploited by animals to become a part of their species.

Were this only true with humans.

We have Benny, a two-year-old Asian elephant who threw out the first pitch to start an exhibition baseball game, wearing an Oakland A's logo.

A farmer in Ontario thought his cows could contribute more to society than just giving milk. So he got the brainstorm to use them as "bullboards" at $500 a side for a year. Advisory: If you or any member of your family is allergic to puns, you may not want to read his pitch for business:

"Do readers skim past your ads? Want to milk the market for all it's worth? If so, it's time you herd about Mediacow."

He said his future plans include looking for something lighter than vinyl to drape over the cows and signs that light up at night.

Another entrepreneur came out with a line of cosmetics for horses. He said it made the animals feel better to have hair and hoof polish on them.

There is no free lunch. We put animals in movies and on TV shows and have them patrol our homes to keep burglars from entering. I even ran across an ad reading, "Uncle Sam Wants Your Dog." It's true, the Department of Defense dog center is looking for a few good canines who want a rewarding career in the military. Requirements are: four legs, at least part German shepherd, rott-weiler, or Bouvier des Flandres.

Must be one to four years old, male or female, and at least twenty-one inches tall at the shoulder and a minimum of fifty pounds.

Must have owner's consent.

What about the dog's consent?

And if someone had told me a couple of bulldogs would have a shotgun wedding, complete with the bride in virginal white and the groom in tails and a silk top hat, I'd have increased my medication.

It seems that just before the annual dog show, the female turned up pregnant. She had been artificially impregnated by the minister, who didn't show up. (He had also impregnated one of the bridesmaids.) So someone had to do the right thing and marry the girl.

As the owner of the dogs said, "I think the groom could care less. He was excited when the breeding happened, but after that he doesn't seem to care. Typical male."

And if you think that's bizarre, a city council in Stanfield, Oregon, found an old ordinance on its books that banned public sex between animals. It carried fines of $5 to $100 or jail terms of two to twenty-five days or both. For the owners, not the animals.

The law, originally passed to control the city's animal population, caused a councilman to observe, "What are you supposed to do, rent them a motel room?"

Humans never seem to be happy with wild animals the way they are. They must be domesticated. They put diapers on their poodles, dress elephants in tutus, have dogs walk on their hind legs, and put fish in aquariums to decorate pediatricians' offices, complete with little castles. We watch chickens dance for corn, monkeys do back flips for loose change, and cats dance for food. If you're an animal who lives in the White House, you have your own literary agent and write a best-seller.

When it comes to exploitation, we have no shame. An earthworm named Willie (we always give them human names) was bought by a man who would dip him in paint and drop him on a canvas. When he had wiggled enough, the man lifted him off and dipped him in another color. In two years the worm did two hundred paintings at $100 a pop. I'm guessing here, but I bet the earthworm didn't see a dime of it.

There is a living and dying cycle in the wild. It runs the gamut from the tortoise, whose life span is about 138 years, to the other end of the spectrum, the mole, which lives only 3 years because his teeth wear out and he starves to death.

Despite our own inadequate health plan system to extend life, we are turning our attention to animals. What can we do to mess them up?

Veterinarians are worried about teeth hygiene. (I wonder if Willie the earthworm had a retirement plan?) They are also concerned about anorexia in dogs, obesity in birds, and respiratory problems in horses.

The hottest health topic in the animal kingdom is the use of Prozac to treat destructive or antisocial disorders.

The *Wall Street Journal* ran a front-page headline, "Listening to Prozac: Bow Wows! I Really Love the Mailman."

Frankly, I can't tell when dogs are depressed. It's hard to read their emotions. We had a dog who for years refused to go outside when we had three bathrooms and wall-to-wall carpeting inside. Whenever he had to "go," he simply lifted his leg on my favorite chair and went.

I took him to a vet who knew about animal behavior and asked him what to do about it. He said, "Sell the chair."

Frankly, I wouldn't want to represent my species in a zoo. It's a tough room. People have paid a fee and are standing there with whining kids who want a hot dog, and they expect you to do something.

Some of us aren't gymnasts, so we can't swing from tires. The audience has seen so much human sex on TV, that's a bore. Watching someone eat or scratch himself isn't a big turn-on either. A little violence gets attention, but there's more of it on the outside of the cage than on the inside.

I hope the guy has a big finish.

25

In Africa, a monkey called the vervet has been studied extensively for communication skills. This species has at least ten sounds in its vocabulary that warn of imminent danger. They use a different alarm for lion, snakes, and so on. But their phrases command attention.

Humans have an entire vocabulary of phrases that can make your blood run cold. This is just a sampling.

"We Can Only Stay Three Weeks."

The houseguests from hell are a constant threat to those of us who live in the Sunbelt. Twenty-one days with a woman who uses the bathroom like she has it in escrow and a husband who refuses to quit smoking because "I could get hit by a beer truck tomorrow." (How can I help?)

That's twenty-one days during which sixty-three meals are served, five thousand miles are put on the car to show them a petting zoo, a power plant, and thirty-five gift shops. Houseguests never share the same politics, like the same TV shows, eat the same food, or keep the same hours as you.

The late British Prime Minister Winston Churchill purportedly loved to visit the White House in Washington, D.C., where he would roam the halls dressed only in an unlit cigar.

But it was a big house.

"Do You Have Health Insurance?"

Before "Hello."

Before "I am bleeding to death."

Before "Do you validate?"

You have to answer the question. If you give the right answer you are rewarded with a cot and attention from someone medical. If you give the wrong answer, you are asked to take a seat and wait, and you will spend whatever time you have left of your life watching people talk to a person behind a glass panel.

You cannot use the same excuses for not having insurance as you used to use for not having your homework: "The dog peed on it." "My brother wrapped his gum in it." "A tornado touched down on our dining room table."

Give them a Paul Anka fan club membership card.

With the reputation hospital computers have for getting things screwed up, no one will ever know the difference.

"Mr. Block, We Are Being Audited."

I don't care who goes with me to the audit—H or R, but I want one of you by my side.

Audits are scary. In the past I have been challenged for declaring visits from my family under medical expenses. Actually, they make me very sick until they leave. What's to understand about that?

One year I was questioned because my entertainment expenditures totaled $22.95.

"What are you? A shut-in?" asked the agent.

"I don't have the income for frills," I said. "A pizza for seven people who come over to watch the Super Bowl is as good as it gets."

My husband is concerned with my record-keeping. I don't keep any. He says we are going to wind up like Willie Nelson, with our friends staging car washes and garage sales to keep us out of jail. Bombeck Aid, so to speak. I think we should direct our paychecks to the IRS. We never see them. They send us a check to live on. We all come out ahead.

"Do You Have Another Credit Card?"

It's every plastic card holder's nightmare. You are at the head of the line when you give the salesperson your item of purchase and your credit card.

You fight not to watch her face too intently, as this creates suspicion. She stares at the computer as if it's a bad tarot card and keeps pushing buttons. The line behind you has now figured out you're a deadbeat. You didn't even keep up the interest payments.

You rummage through your purse for another card, dropping on the floor your AARP membership (now they'll think you're senile), your list of allergies, and your card from I. Magnin, which hasn't been in business for over a year, but it's a status thing.

You give her a second credit card that you have not used in three years and expect the computer to laugh out loud and say, "You want me to do *what?*"

As you leave, a condescending salesperson suggests you contact the credit office. I would rather jump from a bungee cord attached to the wart on Lincoln's face at Mount Rushmore than visit the credit office.

You look at the people in line who are staring at you. You figure you'll never see those people again. You are probably wrong.

"Would You Mind Saying a Few Words?"

The number one fear of humans is the idea of standing up before an audience and saying a few words. It doesn't matter if it's a marriage toast, a bar mitzvah tribute, grace over a dead turkey, or a welcome to the incoming president of the Pee Wee Herman fan club. It's enough to make you breathe into a brown paper bag to keep from passing out.

There is a strong correlation between public speaking and bladder control. I have never known a speaker who has not postponed the opening of the program while he goes to the bathroom one last time. That is why professionals always insist on a pitcher of water nearby. They are dehydrated. When you are addressing a roomful of strangers who aren't laughing or taking notes, the inside of lips turn into Velcro and attach themselves to the teeth, making it impossible to form words.

Occasionally, once a speaker is on his feet, it is difficult to get him to sit down. He has not conquered fear. He is having an out-of-body experience. If and when he returns to earth, he notices half of the room is paging the other half and a few are playing with the melted candles.

In order to sell a book, authors are called upon to give impromptu speeches at a moment's notice. In Pittsburgh on a talk show, a caller wanted to know what I thought about the Pirates. I said I rarely thought about them. If I sold five books after that show I was lucky.

"It's Just Hair. It'll Grow Out."

Beware of hairdressers who do not allow you to face the mirror while they are cutting your hair. A bad haircut grows at the rate of half an inch every three years. You cannot curl it, tame it, or beat it into submission with mousses and sprays. It is there every morning, zinging in fifteen directions. Get over it. It's just a bad hair year.

"How Would You Like to Know Your Grandchild Better?"

If this is spoken by your divorced daughter who is standing by the door with a packed suitcase and airline tickets to California, watch your answer.

Remember, you can lead a fifty-seven-year-old body to motherhood, but you can't make it stay awake.

Probably the most sobering announcement you can hear is, "Guess what? I'm going on the Jenny Jones show to talk about my weird childhood."

For the first two years of a child's life, we spend every waking hour trying to get the child to communicate. Then we spend the rest of our lives trying to figure out how we can reverse the process.

26

The vet noted that Buddy, a dachshund,
had thinning hair on his back.
The doctor said Buddy was going bald because
"intact" (not neutered) males sometimes lose their
hair in that area due to the production of
testosterone. The doctor suggested Buddy's condition
might improve if he was neutered.

Talk about a trade-off!

Soldiers in the battle to conquer baldness have used every weapon in science's arsenal. You can't watch TV without the interruption of a commercial urging men to massage their scalps with a special cream for ninety days, sow hair plugs over their bald spots and eventually harvest a crop of hair, or spring for a rug that comes out of the swimming pool when you do.

I saw a man recently who had a "before" picture

showing him bald and an "after" picture in which he looked like a Chia Pet with a bad haircut.

Men are forever conscious of losing their hair. They check it daily like they're measuring a first down in the Super Bowl. Panic sets in when the forehead extends beyond the top of the head.

Usually, the first thing men do when they find their hair disappearing is to grow a ponytail down their backs. It's a guy thing that makes a statement. "I still have hair. It just won't take direction." Others will grow a single strand of hair that is thirty-six inches in length. Then they will do creative things with it like coil it around until it stops in the center with a thin bang.

Balding men without imagination wear baseball caps to work, parties, and formal weddings, hoping no one will notice.

If a poll were taken among women, I think balding men would be surprised. Being without hair is rather sexy. It brings out a man's eyes, skin, and good teeth, if he has them. If a man has none of the above, he should work as a ski instructor or in a hard-hat area.

Michael Jordan did a lot for baldness. Entire basketball teams have shaved their heads and "the guy with the hair" is the player who isn't cool.

In the animal kingdom of baldees, there are a variety of styles that are inspired. There's the Lou Gossett Jr. porpoise look, in which you don't know where his body ends or his head begins. There's the sage grouse with little points that look like the Statue of Liberty on a rainy day. And of course the baboon who had the misfortune to go bald on the wrong end.

Women have finally admitted to themselves that gravity always wins. You cannot bargain with it, stop it, or have a friend carry it around for you. You may do a bit of tinkering with nips, tucks, and sucks, but generally you have to learn to live with it.

Men are going to have to accept the fact that genetics is a heavy contributor to their lives. There's not a lot you can do with that either.

I'm an optimist. I figure we have developed patches to stop smoking, curb appetite, give us hormones, control moments in which we conceive, eliminate motion sickness, and, yes, even bolster testosterone levels. (And we all want the world to see that patch, don't we?)

Life is full of tough decisions, Buddy. Do we opt for a world where we can have a great body at age 102, but can't be farther than three feet from a restroom? Do we vote in favor of a back full of healthy hair but could care less if anyone runs their fingers through it?

There's another option—have it all shaved off, and learn how to make hook shots!

27

The northern jacana bird dazzles everyone who watches him walk on water. He is called the Jesus Christ bird. Actually, he isn't walking on water at all. His long toes are wrapped around floating vegetation. Many men have used the same trick for years.

In the mid-nineties a men's movement hit this country with all the force of two marshmallows colliding in midair. It produced a couple of bestsellers, *Iron John* by Robert Bly and *Fire in the Belly* by Sam Keen. The entire crusade lasted about fifteen minutes. Frankly, it was all a big bust because there was nothing men needed that they didn't already have. It was like Donald Trump making out his Christmas list.

What were they going to ask for? Pay equal to that received by women?

A sixty-five-hour week?

Twenty-four-hour maternity leave?

A few of the male activists actually went on retreats, beating drums, bonding, and networking. Only *Saturday Night Live!* took note of this momentous event.

The basis for the movement was that men of the fifties had fallen into a pattern. They worked and supported the family, were supposed to love football, tinkered with their cars, and installed automatic garage doors on the weekend. There was no time for interaction with their children or a male presence. They felt dominated by women. They were not happy warriors.

Men set out to solve the problem. They self-induced male menopause. That is to say, at mid-life they got contact lenses, had their hair restyled, wore gold necklaces and $50 sunglasses, bought spa memberships, and left their wives for girls half their ages. That got them alimony payments and an apartment by themselves. Now instead of seeing their children nightly, they had visitation rights every other weekend.

Men joined the ranks of male elephants, otters, turtles, whales, sharks, grizzly bears, and cheetahs, to name a few, who impregnated females and said, "Sayonara, baby."

Some of the men who split figured out kids were like waffles. Pitch the first one and go on to the second, which will not stick and turns out better. They used their young wives to start another family, but this time it was different.

The kids were born in mangers. Imagine still being

able to "have it" at their age. They wore their baby pictures like Olympic medals. They had the time and money to indulge them. They rarely talked about the thirty-two- and thirty-five-year-old offspring who had made them grandfathers five times.

Between men's and women's movements, relationships took some strange turns. Women got to join the Rotary Club and men got to pay the rent on houses they didn't even have keys for.

Women got jobs selling real estate and cosmetics door-to-door, and men got to empty bedpans as nurses and to teach in nursery schools.

But some things didn't change. For women, love was never letting the toilet tissue supply run out. It was cooking the meals, helping the kids with homework, doing the laundry, packing the lunches, changing the sheets, and staying home from work with a sick child.

Men could still walk on water. They could fix a car that wouldn't run, take the squeak out of a door, be smart at math, beat everyone at tennis, and say that everything was going to be all right and be believed.

They had a garage full of tools that could have been surgical instruments for all they knew about them. They couldn't balance a checkbook if their lives depended on it. In truth, they were afraid of snakes, cried during *Bambi* and pretended they'd rubbed salt in their eyes from the popcorn, and released the hood on a rental car when they thought it was the brake.

Some were Ricky Ricardo, who was lord and master of the household, and when he said Lucy couldn't get a job in show business, he meant it. Some were Ralph Kramden, who was king of a castle that should have been condemned. Yet he ate dinner while Alice stood nearby and watched while he forgave her for something she didn't do.

The nineties gave birth to the term "quality time." Compared to what, no one really knew, but they loved saying that's what they spent with their children.

The female shrew, a small mouselike creature, lives in a sex-challenged atmosphere in which she gives birth to half a dozen babies every four months and keeps herself on the brink of starvation while she provides food for everyone else, which means she has to run faster and kill more.

The male shrew is oblivious. He is probably in a field somewhere beating on a rock and searching for the inner warrior within him.

The female shrew usually ends up killing him.

28

In the animal kingdom, like marries like.
They tend to mate with the species
who look and act just like them.

It's hard to believe, but the same happens with humans. Studies show couples resemble each other significantly in physical features. It's called natural selection.

I can hear the cries of dissent from women who say, "Get outta here. I don't begin to resemble a three-day growth of beard, wallowing a toothpick in his mouth, and a stomach that hangs over a belt just above the knees."

Those are external things. Genetically, you are pretty much like the mammal you married. How many women do you know who are married to a Neanderthal? (Okay, half a dozen—tops.)

Mixed marriages are tough. Even in the animal

world. A moose called Joshua (who names these animals?) was attracted to a Hereford cow back in the eighties in Vermont. The romance cooled down when the moose's antlers fell off and his libido (sex drive) diminished. If your husband lost his hair and his libido on the same day, you'd drop him like a bad habit and marry your own kind.

Sometimes animals in the wild and humans conduct courtships in similar ways. An Adelie penguin travels two hundred miles to reach rookeries where female penguins breed. He drops a stone in front of one of them, and if she accepts it with a bow, they mate.

Same thing with our species. A man drops a gem in front of us and we have it appraised. If the rock is worth what we think it is, it's a go.

A male scorpion offers his bride-to-be a substantial amount of food before she consents to mate. Single women have known for a long time that there is no free lunch.

A lot of studies have been done on how the female human predator goes about landing her mate. It is noted that she goes to the bathroom twice as often as men— just to be noticed. She also does a little "scouting" on the trip. She shrugs her shoulders a lot, which is a sign of harmlessness. Her playfulness and childish behavior in the courting period is the same as that of the gray wolf.

Other times, we're not so close. The beaver, for example, makes mud pies perfumed by its own urine and leaves them in a prominent place to attract a lady friend. It's a wonder they're not extinct.

To figure out if a male has "staying power," animals figure the courtship dance is a real test. The Laysan albatross, for example, performs eight different steps.

That's when I realized my marriage was doomed. At the wedding when the orchestra played "Our Love Is Here to Stay," my groom took fifteen minutes to button his coat. I should have realized then the man could not move his feet.

The stones . . . the flirting . . . the dinners . . . none of that mattered. I've seen men wearing cowboy hats bigger than a satellite dish, who look like they can't remember where they parked their car, line dance until they drop. Their routines are intricate blends of backward glides, twirls, and boots crossing at the knees. That's the man I should have married.

They were playing a simple waltz the other night. I asked my husband, "Do you want to dance?"

"It's a fad," he said. "In another ten years no one will be dancing."

"You said that about red meat and electricity."

A courtship ritual that I find appealing is practiced by the bowerbirds of New Guinea and Australia. To attract a mate, they build elaborate homes out of bottle caps, fishing lures, grasses, twigs, thongs, buckles, and anything else that man has discarded. A female bowerbird knows what she is getting into: a palatial roof over her head and no mortgage payments.

I didn't marry Bob Vila. I didn't even marry Tim Allen of *Home Improvement*. When my mate found the fuse box in our first house, you would have thought

Indiana Jones had found the treasures of the Lost Ark.

I don't know of too many couples who come back from their honeymoons to the house of their dreams. They first have to pass a marriage test called "arrange the furniture." Newlyweds have different ideas on what a house should look like and how it should function:

> To a male, a nail in the wall to hold anything is considered the rape of a virgin.

> He should be able to put an ugly chair that bangs against the wall when it reclines and a reading lamp and a table in his domain, which is six feet from the TV set.

> The TV tuner is a part of the chair.

> On moving day, the piano is moved to a spot, never to be moved again.

> A light should never be illuminated when no one is in the room.

A marriage is a lot more interesting if the rules are challenged.

I want to reject the theory of couples resembling each other as the years go by, but a picture I saw a few years ago haunts me. A couple who were about to celebrate their fiftieth wedding anniversary were pictured in the newspaper.

They stared straight ahead, their shoulders barely

touching. Both had short, thinning hair that revealed pink scalps. Their skins were smooth. If neither of them shaved for three weeks, no one would notice. There was puffiness beneath two pairs of eyes. Both folded their arms on breasts that somehow had leveled out to the same size. His chest muscles had flattened out; her boobs had dropped. They wore glasses rimmed in gold. Neither wore makeup.

They had physically blended into the same person!

Is that scary or what? Maybe it wouldn't be so bad if you were married to Tony Curtis, but what are the odds of that happening?

Monogamy is rare in the animal kingdom. It's even rarer in the human kingdom. The jackdaw bird pairs off at one year of age and remains faithful for the rest of his life. Their union could last as long as sixty-five years. Swans stay together for life; so do coyotes and golden eagles.

On the other end of the spectrum you have tigers, who are together only two or three days, but they mate over 160 times. It gives new meaning to the list held by a magnet on the refrigerator door, "Things to Do Today."

I looked in the mirror the other day. The reflection showed a woman who looked like she had just walked into a wrecking ball.

Would I be stupid enough to marry someone who looked like me? When the Pope wears plaids.

29

Man is the only creature endowed with the power of laughter; is he not also the only one that deserves to be laughed at?

—*Fulke Greville*

The above quote is one I'd always subscribed to until one day when I was putting on a pair of size A pantyhose (fits 110–120 pounds) over my size C torso (150–infinity) and saw my dog laughing. His tongue was hanging out, his gums and teeth were exposed, and I think he even made nose noises. It shot a hole in the first part of Greville's observation. Now, every time I see a porpoise, I want to ask, "What are you laughing at?" Crocodiles have a smile I've seen on the face of every lawyer I've ever met.

Hyenas laugh themselves into a coma over a few lousy, unappetizing leftovers.

There are lots of animals in show business. Lipizzaners prance on their hind legs, and bears pose for pictures. But they're trained to do that. Anyone can dress a monkey in a diaper and put him on a tricycle.

But are there any real comics in the animal kingdom? Is there anyone out there who would cause Seinfeld to lose a night's sleep?

Bobby Berosini swears he is the straight man for five orangutans. The trainer contends he does not coach or train the apes. From the moment the act starts, the animals own the stage. They interact with the audience whenever they feel like it and occasionally change the act.

Whatever they're doing, they're doing well at it, entertaining five hundred people twice nightly, six days a week. "It's like watching five performing poets," says Berosini, "although their humor is a little coarse."

Today's human comedians (male and female) have three standard topics in their routines: airline food, sexual ineptness, and losing weight.

Actually, the orangutans are a bit more traditional. They go for the visuals. Like the quick fall in the Clint Eastwood film, *Every Which Way But Loose.* Clint would look at the ape, point his finger, and say, "Bang bang," and the animal would drop to the ground like a stone. It's shades of Milton Berle and Red Skelton.

Having humor transcend a common language is tough. The longest night I ever spent was watching a comedy show in Rio performed in Portuguese.

I don't think everyone in the animal kingdom does comedy. I saw a television commercial for cat food once in which a cat wore a striped coat and a top hat and carried a cane. He wasn't smiling. He looked like he was going to call his agent as soon as the director yelled, "Cut!" In fact, I have never seen a cat smile. They're too cool.

When I worked for *Good Morning America* we thought it would be fun if I went to see Andrew Lloyd Webber's stage hit *Cats* with Morris, the highest-paid cat in television.

Morris never did get into the program. He looked bored, like he wanted to be anywhere else. We got great seats and I put the animal on the aisle. His trainer said he didn't weigh enough to hold down the seat by himself, so I should hold my knee against his seat to give it weight.

When someone wanted to enter the row, I instinctively stood up and Morris disappeared down the back of the seat like someone had just released the trap on a guillotine. He wasn't hurt. He only looked mean.

The more I told him to lighten up, the worse he got.

As I told *Entertainment Tonight* in an interview about my date, "I've had furrier, shorter, and less talkative escorts, but this one had the personality of a wall."

In the human world there doesn't seem to be a formula for comedians. Some are shy (Bob Newhart), others are insecure (Woody Allen), some are extroverts (Jerry Lewis), some will do anything for attention (Rosie

O'Donnell), others phone in their material from another planet (Robin Williams).

Human comedy material can be quite obscene with hand and finger gestures, like the subtlety of the orang-utan, or squeaky clean, like the Big Bird variety.

But we seem to laugh at the same things—even if they are insensitive and in bad taste.

The enigma I can't figure out is the shark. He's a loner with no friends or social life, is grossly overweight, and has a bad dental plan. He has a perennial smile on his face for no apparent reason.

Go figure.

30

It has taken years of trying to understand animal behavior for researchers to confirm that animals love to play. Grizzlies slide down hills in the snow, elephants whack a ball of sun-baked earth with their trunks, and badgers do somersaults, play leapfrog, and do a shuffle dance a lot like the twist.

Before we sent kids to computer camps and told them they were having a good time, there was imagination among the human species. After all, humans are only animals.

It's Christmas Eve around 3 A.M. My husband is putting together a bicycle with instructions written in Japanese. Two wing nuts are missing. Something is not right. The seat is on the handlebars.

I am struggling to gift wrap a game that my daughter vowed to will herself dead if she didn't get. I went to fifteen stores, only to be told they were sold out. I finally ended up at Nuts R Us and scalped her game from a woman with fifteen watches for sale that ran up to her elbow.

We won't be finished until daylight comes. There are tracks to be laid, batteries to be loaded, stockings to stuff, a dollhouse to assemble.

As usual, we have gone crazy to buy our children's affection. There must be $700 worth of toys under the tree awaiting their squeals of delight.

Cut to Christmas morning. The kids don't know what to do first: pop the plastic bubbles in the wrapping, play in the cardboard box, or gather up all the ribbons and make a "bridal bouquet" out of them.

Two days later, the bicycle has virgin tires and is still under the tree. My son has taken a huge box that held a new coffee table and dragged it to his room. He announces he is "going to the moon in it."

When he doesn't show up for dinner, I check in on him, and he says he has all the supplies he needs and if I wish to speak to him again, it will have to be through mission control.

I remind him to tether himself and occasionally float on down to the bathroom.

We lost something wonderful when little girls stopped making dolls out of clothespins and hollyhocks and graduated to Barbie, who has a change of clothes demanded by her checkered career, which includes stewardess, astronaut, nurse, corporate executive, professional ice skater, servicewoman, and docent for the Bra Museum in Los Angeles.

The little boys who used to crouch behind an evergreen with a bandana around their heads and a pirate's saber made out of cardboard now sit in front of a TV set with $60 games that can terminate the world with one click of the finger. I supported the parents who seemed to think that toys should be challenging and improve the mind. Now I'm inclined to wonder, what's wrong with mindless activities?

I read a story about a thousand-pound polar bear lumbering toward a dog in mid-November. Since the ice had not formed and the open waters prevented bears from hunting seals, he had been virtually fasting for four months.

An hors d'oeuvre was within his grasp.

The dog did what any mentally deficient dog would do in that situation. He wagged his tail, grinned, and actually bowed to the bear. The bear responded in a nonaggressive way and body language that suggested, "Let's play."

For several minutes, dog and bear wrestled and cavorted. The bear at one point completely wrapped himself around the dog and embraced him. Every evening for more than a week, the bear returned to romp and play with the dog in the snow. The hunter and trapper who witnessed this behavior had no explanation for it—only that play is important, as when you call a kid to dinner and he'd rather kick a can down the street than eat. He took a guess that play ranks right up there with food, mating, and developing physically and mentally. Other scientists went even further. They concluded that if play is absent from a child's life or the child is mistreated, his development could be abnormal.

In an animal show on PBS one night, monkeys climbed up a large tree, grabbed a ropelike branch, and swung out over the water before letting go. They clambered out of the water and climbed to an even higher branch than before and repeated the same act. They weren't securing food or looking out for predators. They weren't collecting anything or staking out territories. They were doing only one thing—having a ball.

My mind went back to my childhood. With some regularity we would visit cousins who lived on a farm. There were thirteen kids in the family, and the high point of their year came when the circus PR man rented a spot on their barn for a huge poster and gave them free tickets for the circus.

There were a few slingshots and a couple of ratty-looking homemade dolls in the house—but no toys.

Their favorite fun place was a small river that ran along their property. There was a tree nearby and they'd climb to the top of it, grab a rope, and swing out and drop into the water.

I hated it. The mud oozed between my toes when I got out, the rocks killed my tender feet, and there were crawdads, snakes, and God knows what else in there. This analogy between the monkeys and my cousins is in no way intended to convince you my relatives grew up normal, but surely you can see the similarity between the way they had a good time.

Finding a creative vein in their children is one of the

things that instills pride in parents. A friend of ours once told us the story of finding in the backseat of his station wagon a wonderful crayoned picture his son had drawn at nursery school. He was ecstatic. The colors were bold, there was depth, and the design clearly showed signs of promise. As a surprise for his son, he decided to have it framed. When it was finished, he made a big deal out of the unveiling. He invited the boy to his office and said, "Son, I may not always praise you as often as I should, but I want you to know that I am not unaware of your talents. I shall cherish this picture for the rest of my life. It will hang over my desk."

His son looked up and said, "Why would you want a picture drawn by Jeffy Karcher over your desk? You barely know him."

Not every species agrees on what is a game and what isn't. In the Galápagos, a sea lion pup—the little prankster—will drag an iguana a short distance into a tidepool, release it, let it swim toward shore, then grab it again and drag it back in the pool.

And if that doesn't break you up, think of my cousins, whose idea of fun was to sneak up behind you and pull your legs out from under you.

If my cousins had lived in the wild, there's no doubt, they'd have been eaten first.

31

The cockroach has endured for three hundred million years. It is immune to fire, flood, glaciers, land upheaval, volcanos, insecticides, and radioactivity. There is a rumor that you can destroy it with a hair dryer on high heat. This is not true.

There is not a human being who can match the survival of the cockroach. Occasionally you will read of men or women who top a hundred years or so, but death finally claims them.

There are, however, three foods our species leave behind that refuse to die. They will occupy this earth as long as the cockroach.

A pot of split pea soup not only survived two moves, three power outages, a blizzard, a hundred-year flood, three teenagers, and an exorcist, it multiplied.

My first experience with split pea soup was a gift

from my mother. She made a quart of it one day, and after she and my dad had eaten from it for three months, she asked, "Why don't you take some of it home with you?"

Ordinarily, I do not eat anything that turns green when you cook it and takes off your lipstick when you eat it, but I felt sorry for her. She seemed so desperate. I refrigerated the leftover. The split pea soup wouldn't live and it wouldn't die. I eventually buried it in the backyard, where the grass died and the area turned into a green, soggy mud patch.

Another food that will outlast civilization is the hard roll. These are nondescript rolls that turn to rock two hours after you buy them. If you bite into one, it will heal itself.

I wanted to believe that when a hard roll became stale enough, it was pitched out. This proved not to be true. On a tour through Europe, every morning we were served a continental breakfast. It didn't matter if we were airborne or in a hotel, we got the continental breakfast. It consisted of a glass of juice, a hard roll, a small plastic packet of jelly, and a beverage of our choice.

I personally felt the hard rolls were making me mean. I had mood swings and some days I didn't want to get out of bed. I also suspected they were serving us the same roll in every city we visited, so one morning in Amsterdam I etched my husband's initials in one. Sure enough, on the last night of the tour in Paris, we were dining in a restaurant in the Eiffel Tower when a waiter put a roll beside my husband's plate. The initials WLB stood out like a neon sign. For all I know, it's still circling the globe.

But the ultimate in longevity is the Christmas fruitcake. It is a cake made during the holidays with fruits that make it heavier than the stove it is cooked in.

There is something "different" about people who like fruitcake. They never eat it themselves, but they're absolutely evangelistic about everyone else eating them. I have an aunt who approaches me every year with her favorite fruitcake as a gift. I look her in the eye and say, "Aunt Mildred, I did not like the fruitcake last year. I will not like it this year, and I will not eat it next year. Live with it."

Now, here's another thing I hate about fruitcake bakers. They are never rebuffed. She smiles through the rejection and starts to slice me a piece. "I would have more respect for you, Aunt Mildred, if you would just say, 'Who asked you to eat this cake? It cost me $45 to make and if it were up to me, I'd drop it on your ungrateful foot!'" But no, she forces it into my mouth, and when I spit it out in my hand, she smiles. "Now, isn't that moist?"

My theory is shared by many. There are only four or five fruitcakes making the rounds like a chain letter. If you don't give away your fruitcake before the year is up, something terrible will happen to you.

My belief in this philosophy was reinforced when I read about a fruitcake baked by Fridelia Ford in November 1878 in Berkey, Ohio. According to tradition, she let it set for a year and planned to cut it the following

Thanksgiving. However, she died before this happened and the cake kicked around in the family until 1952 when it found a permanent home with her great grandson, Morgan Ford of Tecumseh, Michigan.

Every year at reunions and special occasions it is trotted out under glass and stared at like a gem in the Hermitage.

In 1966, one of the uncles took a nibble from it and lived for another two years, so it couldn't have been that bad.

Author Diane Lewis, in an effort to preserve the planet, published a small book on ways to recycle your fruitcake. Several suggestions worth nothing are placing a fruitcake in your toilet tank and saving thousands of gallons of water each year, or sending it to geologists to fill in the San Andreas fault to save our West Coast from seismographic destruction.

Any day I expect to see Martha Stewart come out with an entire issue of her magazine devoted to "Beyond Fruitcake."

Fruitcake swimming pools, patios and walls, highways, high-rise buildings, automobile tires, and jewelry.

I have seen enough Roman ruins to know that even their genius at building cities eventually crumbled and faded.

This will not happen with the fruitcake.

As a matter of fact, I have another theory. If one cockroach takes a bite out of Aunt Mildred's 138-fruits-the-longer-it-sits-the-moister-it-gets fruitcake . . . it will die.

32

---

*An animal nutritionist at the Bronx Zoo
is concerned about the cholesterol level
of many of the animals housed there.
So the rhinos are getting their vitamin E,
the toads are being served crickets seasoned with
calcium dust, baby mouse deer get a formula with
extra protein, and fat- and leaf-eating monkeys
and anteaters get their needed dose of fiber.*

The fat police couldn't stand it, could they? They just refused to stand by and watch goats enjoying themselves eating old beer cans and maribou storks eating five-day-old contaminated meat. Oh no, they had to take away the joy of food.

They've done it to humans. I come from a family where everything my mother bought was stamped "one hundred percent sugar," "made with pure cream," and "real butter." Gravy poured from our tap in the kitchen.

Today, I'm going half nuts reading the contents of everything I eat . . . in metric no less. (I thought a gram was a cracker.)

All of my pleasures are gone. I have nothing left to live for. My birthday cakes were clogging my arteries, so I now have a curd loaf drizzled with a topping of wheat germ.

Picnics used to be a mayonnaise and beef orgy. Now we have turkey patties and potato salad moistened with the drops of water from lettuce leaves.

The food industry has made so many substitutions in foods, I don't know what I'm eating anymore.

My husband buys a margarine that won't melt in a skillet. It's true. You deposit a glob of it and the next thing you know it has disappeared into the stove vent. This is not natural.

The fat and fiber Nazis appear out of the woodwork. They point out that if I were on a diet plan of fifteen hundred calories a day, I've already have eaten my limit through August 1998.

They do it through intimidation. I go to a restaurant and order cream of mushroom soup for an appetizer when I feel three pairs of eyes on me. "What was I thinking?" I laugh. "Make that low-sodium bouillon."

When it comes to selecting the salad, I order a Caesar, but to please my table companions I order dressing on the side. (When they're not looking, I down it like it's in a shot glass.)

I want to eat fettucine Alfredo, but I know that if I

order it they would throw a telethon for me. When the dessert cart comes to a stop at our table, my friends look at it as though they're viewing a friend in a mortuary.

If we continue with this madness, we might just as well dine on our handbags.

The lone voice of sanity in all this is premier chef Julia Child, who was quoted as saying in an interview, "Nutritional police will kill gastronomy. Forget the cheap white wine; go to the beef and gin!"

Okay, so maybe the animal kingdom has a few stomach disorders and bad teeth. But they're smart enough to eat when they're hungry. They invented carry-out. When was the last time you heard of a family of wildebeest sitting down under a nice tree having dinner? Bats sleep all day and consume half their weight at night. I relate to that. Even the koala spends most of his waking hours snacking.

I personally believe there are two things you can't mess around with: reproductive cycles and the food chain. It will divide a nation.

I am married to a health disciple. When he sees a bacon bit on a spinach salad, he pales and looks like he has just seen a scorpion crawl up his pants leg. After he isolates it on the side of the plate, he has been known to grab a telephone pad and sketch a clogged artery on it for me to see.

I have great respect for the way animals eat. Even though the finch and the alligator have no tongues or lips, they can still find something—or someone—to dine on.

In all fairness to the nutritionists at the Bronx Zoo

who are trying to change the eating habits of animals, they are doing this because of a study with the Przewalski—a brownish, small, horselike animal. They found a link between a lack of vitamin E and the health of the animal's spinal cord. Some males were unable to mount or mate. Since they've been on vitamins, their breeding efforts have increased. I don't know what this has to do with taking away my enjoyment of pizza.

The other evening I was at a movie when I leaned over and said to my husband, "I'm going to the rest room." I eased out of my seat in the darkness and headed for the snack bar, where I got a Jacuzzi-sized box of buttered popcorn. I slipped outside where I saw the embers of a group of smokers who huddled together like parolees.

"Having a cigarette?" asked the voice of someone I couldn't see in the darkness.

"No," I said, "I'm eating buttered popcorn."

"Don't you know that'll kill you?" said a smoker.

"That's disgusting," said a female voice.

They all moved away from me.

33

When a reindeer pulls a **pulkha** *(sleigh) it is as if he is driving at high speed in a car with no brakes. He has no control or mind of his own. Every few minutes, the animal gets bored with the road and tries to lunge up a snowbank.*

I have managed to stay alive all these years because (*a*) I never eat airline food, and (*b*) I never ride in the car with my grown kids driving it.

When I was teaching the first of my children to drive, I made a promise to God that if He would let me out of that car safely, I would divest myself of all my credit cards and join Mother Teresa in Calcutta.

When children reach the age of sixteen, they discover the meaning of life: car keys. Within minutes after they get their driver's license, they want a car of their own.

He brings one home for your approval. Parts of the

Grand Canyon are only five years older than that car. It's a convertible winter and summer because the top has tears in it that flap in the wind like a Bedouin tent. The windows do not go up or down. When you go over a bump in the road, one headlight goes on; when you go over a second bump, it goes off again. The seat belt is five inches in circumference and fits no one. The car gets four miles to the gallon and should be owned by someone who could afford it—a sheik in Saudi Arabia.

Nothing works in the vehicle—except the tape deck. Its volume can be cranked up to ninety-six decibels, covering six traffic lights.

When you total up the registration and license fees and insurance, it costs three times more than he paid for the car.

"I got a Club for it," he says proudly. "It fits over the steering wheel."

"Why?"

"So no one will steal it."

"The only way anyone is going to steal this car is to break it down and carry it off in a shopping bag."

Their goal in life is to have everything working in the car at the same time. This never happens.

There is always a knock, a squeak, a rumble, a grinding, or smoke pouring out from some opening in the car. His mechanic is right out of *Deliverance*. He only accepts cash.

"I thought you were going to take your car to your mechanic this weekend."

"I can't. It's going to rain."

"What does that have to do with anything?"

"He works on the car in his driveway."

Some naive parents actually believe that when their child gets a car, their lives will be made easier. The child will pick up the cleaning, drop in at the store and pick up a few things, go to the airport for you, drop you off at the beauty shop, or take Grandma to the doctor.

If you believe that, you believe Ivana and Donald Trump actually get together to share a pizza.

You will never see this child again.

From the moment my first driver rolled his car down the driveway to get it started, I knew our bonding was over.

It would be years before he would forgive me for making him the oldest boy in North America who rode a bicycle to school.

My husband was a high school administrator. He said you could always distinguish the teachers' cars from the kids' in the parking lot. The teachers' cars looked like a graveyard for Volkswagens. The bumper stickers supported the teachers union and had signs that read, BABY ON BOARD. There was a hole where the radios had been and the antennas had been bent double.

Sometimes I wonder what the animal kingdom must think as they see humans crouched in cars that belch carbon monoxide, stall and sputter, and become such an important part of our lives.

And when humans have great distances to travel, they board a large bird and are at their destination in hours.

I can't help but think of the penguins. If one ran away from home, with those awkward baby steps it would take him three years to get to the shoreline. And yet every year they travel nine hundred miles from home to Antarctic rookeries to mate.

If humans had to travel that far on foot, we would have become extinct a million years ago.

34

Although many wild animals are seen throughout the day—birds, cats, cockroaches, and hippos—most are regarded as nocturnal. They come out at night to hunt for food. Mosquitoes come out to suck the blood out of sleeping humans.

The smart thing about nocturnal animals in the wild is that they do not enter into mixed relationships. A badger would never join up with another badger who was a "day person," and a hyena would not hang out with another hyena who conked out on him at nine in the evening.

Humans, unfortunately, think they can overcome the differences of their twenty-four-hour clocks.

I married a man with the insides of a hamster forty-six years ago. He functions throughout the day—but not well. When the sun goes down, his body goes on alert.

He zips out of his BarcaLounger and starts to forage for food and drink. The TV tuner flips channels like a Charlie Chaplin movie on fast-forward. Sometimes he goes to the garage and turns on his saws or fiddles with the lawn mower until he gets it started. He flips on the radio for "company."

He nudges the dog out of a sound sleep, and the dog eventually starts barking to be let out.

He calls people in time zones where they have been asleep for three hours to ask, "What time is it there?"

With his stomach full and the night behind him, he makes a noisy entrance into the bathroom, where he flushes, hums, and gargles like a volcano ready to blow.

He hits the bed with a bounce, wraps the entire king-size blanket around his body, and dozes off. The alarm will go off in two hours.

It's something you don't discuss before you get married—and you should. It's like being married to a man who is hooked up to a NordicTrack from midnight to 5 A.M.

Some people say they can't tell the difference between a day person and a night person. Grow up! All you have to do is go to an overnight supermarket and it will hit you right between the eyes.

They slip into the store at some ungodly hour in a wrinkled warm-up suit, no socks, and sunglasses even though the sun set four hours ago.

They grab the first cart by the door, even if it has a piece of lettuce caught in the seat.

Their first words to the cashier are, "What time do you close?"

They never squeeze fruit or read labels. They just toss the stuff into the cart.

There's an inattentiveness about nighttime shoppers, like they just popped in during a commercial for a bag of chips and a six-pack. They don't care what they buy. They just stand in front of a bunch of boxes that say "Just add water," close their eyes, and grab one.

They will buy a tabloid at the checkout even if the headline reads "Why Roseanne Cried on Her Wedding Night" and they know the answer will be "Room service was closed."

Most nocturnal animals are unwilling to follow eating patterns set by *Homo sapiens*. This is too bad because wild animals are basically weird. The giraffe gets up at 6 in the morning if he wants to have breakfast by 9 because the food has a long way to travel. One meal a day is enough for a lion and would be for all of us if all we did all day was swat flies. The koala bear eats all day and all night on a diet of eucalyptus leaves. He rarely stops eating the evergreen, which contains medicinal oils and is addictive. He lives with a buzz on. A boa constrictor can live off one large prey for two weeks. I don't want to go into that.

Normal humans consume three meals a day in some kind of pattern. Except nocturnal people and Frenchmen. For some reason, they put nine or ten hours between lunch and dinner. Just because animals dine fashionably late, I see no reason to stand around a party eating bait off a Ritz cracker in anticipation of a meal that will be served at 10:30 at night. It's unnatural.

Depending on which genes are dominant, children can go either way. All of ours were born nocturnal. As newborn infants they ate all night and slept all day. As they grew older, I got up when they were coming in went to bed when they were going out.

Sadly, humans are losing their work-all-day/sleep-all-night patterns. More and more of our businesses and social pleasures are staying open twenty-four hours a day to accommodate the night people. They can bank, bowl, shop, pray, do their laundry, see a movie, eat and drink, get married, gamble, fly to New York, have a baby, or have their spouses arrested. The services are all there for them.

Our kids once owned a hamster called Ben. Ben was a real charmer. During the day he would coil up in a ball at the side of his cage with all the personality of a dustball. You couldn't wake him up. At night when I was in bed, I could hear him running around that squeaky wheel like he was leading the pack at Boston. It was a wheel to nowhere, but those little feet would go nonstop all night long.

I don't know if Ben was male or female. Didn't matter. That hamster and my husband had a marriage made in heaven.

35

*The proboscis monkey resembles a lot of other
simian species except for one thing. As the adult
male matures, his nose never stops growing. He has
one of the biggest noses in the history of nature. By
the time he reaches full size, it gets in the way when
he tries to eat, and he often has to resort to using one
hand for climbing because he needs the other free to
push aside the branches so they don't hit his nose.
The natives of Borneo—cut off from civilization—
used to call him the White Man.*

*L*et's be honest here. For every animal roaming around
the jungle, flying in the air, or cruising through the
seas, there is a human counterpart who bears a strong
resemblance on shore.

The proboscis monkey isn't the only one with a forty-
pound honker. In addition to the fictional Cyrano de

Bergerac and Pinocchio, real people also have prominent nasal appendages—Karl Malden and the late Jimmy Durante.

And who has not blanched at the story of J. P. Morgan, whose wealth was exceeded only by the size of his nose.

On the day he was to come for tea at the home of Dwight Morrow, the Morrow children were drilled on the subject of tact and manners. Under no circumstances were they to mention his conspicuous nose.

Under great stress, Mrs. Morrow went through the motions of pouring tea for her guest, occasionally tossing a threatening look at her daughters. They stared, but they said nothing.

With a great sigh of relief, Mrs. Morrow smiled at her guest and said, "And now, Mr. Morgan, will you have one or two lumps of sugar in your nose?"

Many humans who have pets vehemently deny that they own animals who resemble them, but it's true. Never is this more evident than at a dog show competition, where there are a number of breeds running with their owners.

A woman who has already lost the battle of gravity will have a basset hound on a leash. A crabby-looking, portly man will lead around a bulldog. And a woman who has bangs down to her nose and never shaves her legs will display a sheepdog.

I must admit, every time I see a rhino from the rear with those little short legs holding it up, I get a bit uncomfortable. If I don't stop with the root beer floats, that is my future.

What has happened throughout the years is that humans were getting dangerously close to looking like animals in the wild. Just shaving our legs and our armpits wasn't enough, so plastic surgery was invented to put a little distance between us.

We had excess hair removed from our faces, reduced the size of our ears, pumped the fat out of our thighs, and had our noses bobbed.

Of course, we have the advantage of clothes. Few animals (with the exception of snakes) have a change of outfit.

There are still similarities between the way animals and humans look. I saw Queen Elizabeth in a hat exactly like the headpiece of the cassowary bird of Papua New Guinea. Michael Jordan has legs comparable only to those of a whooping crane. Everyone has an accountant with eyes like a bald eagle. In a singles bar, the rows of spandex predators look like dolphins at Sea World. I've seen beards on men so full, they could hibernate and no one would be surprised.

I don't tell this to many people, but I went on a banana diet once . . . nothing but bananas all day long. By the end of two weeks, I found myself swinging across the kitchen by my arms, grabbing a banana off the shelf, and eating it without peeling it. It doesn't take long to return to your roots.

Since the natives of Borneo had never seen a white man, it is interesting that they would have thought this monkey with the reddish-brown body and a pinkish-white face (which turns red when it is excited or over-heated) could be human.

Maybe they had heard that the white man put his nose into everyone else's business, and it required an industrial-strength nose. Another theory is that the nose was a sign of virility that males use to attract members of the opposite sex. However, an equal number of experts felt it enhanced their voices—described as nasal, what else?—and was the monkeys' way of asserting their territory.

So the Borneo natives developed a fondness for the proboscis monkey. Roasted. Talk about a negative tourism move.

I don't know when the first white man set foot on Borneo soil, but the natives must have looked at him in his Banana Republic attire and his pith helmet, studied his face closely, and observed, "Bad nose job."

36

In Paris, a man ordered lobster and questioned its freshness. The waiter thrust it under the customer's nose and ordered him to smell it.

The lobster seized the man's nose and took off a portion of it. In court, the customer was awarded a settlement and the owner was fined $8 for not keeping a dangerous animal under control.

Scientists frown on any tendency of writers to anthropomorphize the animal kingdom. They can verify their eating and sex habits and their reproduction cycles, but when it comes to human attributes, they draw the line.

I think animals have attitudes just like people.

Every time I read of a prison riot in which men and women are frustrated and don't want to be there, I think of Octavia, the octopus who was the big attraction a few years ago at the Cabrillo Marine Aquarium in L.A.

She was the first giant octopus to be displayed at the aquarium, but not everyone was happy with it. A group of animal activists said Octavia's home was too small, and Octavia agreed with them.

One night, with her powerful tentacles she pulled the plug—literally. When she sucked the pipe from the drain, the water flowed out faster than it came in. The cause of death was listed as "octopus automutilation syndrome."

Frankly, I don't think Octavia thought that one through. The octopus—perhaps the most intelligent of all sea dwellers with the exception of marine mammals—let her attitude get in the way.

Unlike wild animals, humans have a way of dealing with their attitudes. They're called lawyers. If Octavia had been of the domestic phylum, she wouldn't have had to pull her own plug. She'd have summoned a Dr. Kevorkian to do it for her, and the courts would have to bear the responsibility for the action. The results would have been the same, but having a lawyer to plead your case gets people's attention.

Lawyers in the nineties have become the most influential professionals in our society. They bring down decisions on who gets to visit the children and who receives alimony and the Suns season tickets in the event of divorce. They decide who's responsible for selling us a lemon, how to make peace with the IRS, and what kind of community service we have to perform. A couple even sued over the rights to a frozen embryo.

Going to court will get you on the cover of *Time,* win you a book contract and a movie-of-the-week, and attract paparazzi like mosquitoes to ankles. Zsa Zsa Gabor was quoted as saying, "I hope I have enough dresses to cover the length of my trial."

There are two things to be considered when choosing attorneys: Have they been on David Letterman? Does the nanny for their children have a green card?

This has become the decade of the protection of citizens' rights. Television ads tell you how easy it is to make a pot of money for your "pain and suffering." In California, there are special ads for lawyers who deal only in motorcycle altercations.

The courts are bulging with nuisance suits that eventually create a new level of millionaires. They didn't inherit a company and they didn't win the lottery. They just found a fingernail in their diet drink and voilà! . . . A company pays big for the "pain and suffering."

A $700,000 suit for compensatory damages and $1.3 million in punitive damages went to court because a cup of coffee was served too hot, the lid was not secured, and the customer suffered burns.

I met a friend of mine in a mall parking lot the other day. She was driving a BMW.

"When did you get a BMW?" I asked.

"Oh, you didn't hear? My hairdresser turned my hair orange."

"It's always been orange."

"No, this was a real Halloween orange. I had a lot of pain and suffering, so we settled out of court. I guess you heard about Becky."

"No, what happened to her?"

"She found a piece of glass in her laxative. She's always been a lucky stiff. A few years ago, a dry cleaner shrunk her cashmere sweater."

"That's too bad."

"No, that's good. Today she owns the company."

"Wait a minute," I said. "Are you telling me if a restaurant served me an anchovy on my pizza and I'm allergic to anchovies, I could sue?"

"A good lawyer could make you a rich woman."

I have never seen so many Americans who are angry at someone or something. Not since the vigilantes have we had so many people armed and ready to carry out Wild West justice. The O. J. Simpson trial has turned into a cottage industry.

Friends of the couple have book and TV movie contracts. One has a 900 number to talk about his relationship with O. J. Kato, the house sitter, has a SAG card and became the darling of the media after his testimony. The jury is bored and hostile toward one another because they can't agree on what TV shows to watch while they're sequestered. A couple of them have quit and appeared on the evening news and tabloid shows.

Some would argue, what do animals have to have an attitude about?

The mole rat is the only rodent born without a fur coat. With a good lawyer, someone would pay for that little oversight.

And what about the St. Bernard with grounds for an

affirmative action suit? For centuries these animals dug people out of the snow and were a breed synonymous with rescue. Now St. Bernards have been dismissed and replaced by German shepherds, whose agile movements and sensitive noses make them more effective in sniffing out missing skiers and climbers.

And what attorney wouldn't salivate over a class action suit by red ants. In 1810, they were taken to be slave labor in an ant colony. The practice still exists today.

The law of the jungle is very simple and easy to understand:

Never eat anyone larger than you.

If you're not a tree climber, do not climb trees.

Know your territory. If the urine is not yours, you're not home.

Avoid headlights and agents who want to make you a star.

There is a time to fight and a time to run. Know the difference.

If a human attorney puts a sign on a hut that reads, "Animal Law a Specialty," eat him.

37

The pterosaur dinosaur discovered in Texas is possibly the largest flying animal who ever lived. The species roamed the earth over sixty million years ago before becoming extinct.

The brain of the stegosaurus was smaller than a nerve knot on its spine.

In the next millennium, an army of archeologists will search for clues to what happened to our civilization. Why did they die? How did they expire? What led to their disappearance from the face of the earth?

Their quest will lead them to the vast parking lot outside a humongous shopping mall in Bloomington, Minnesota. There they will find a mother lode of skeletons and artifacts. As they piece together the evidence, they will concur that death was due to terminal confusion, dehydration, and the inability of shoppers to find their cars. They just dropped in their tracks and died.

Their ages will be determined by their shopping bags boasting the names of stores that went into Chapter 11 hundreds of years ago.

It's frightening, but like the dinosaur, that is probably how our civilization will go.

In the eighties shopping malls began to appear big time. By the nineties malling had not only become a verb, it had become a way of life. A classified newspaper ad with a house to sell didn't list how far it was from good schools or the fire department. It proudly proclaimed: "Two miles from the mall."

And then, in the summer of 1992, a voice was heard in Bloomington, Minnesota: "Build a mall—and they will come."

At a cost of $625 million, the mall covers 4.2 million square feet. There are fourteen movie screens, six supper clubs, a seven-acre Knott's Berry Farm, a seventy-foot-high roller coaster, and four hundred specialty stores. (Just a guess, but there are probably forty parking spaces.)

No one has to tell me malls are designed to hold you captive. Even when I look at the map under glass that says, "You are here," I don't know where I am. One day in the complex I met a pathetic woman who tapped me on the arm and said, "What day is it?" "Wednesday," I said. She remained stoic and added, "What year?"

Here was a woman who had been in the mall so long, she had missed the Vietnam War, Oprah's weight loss, and Michael Jackson's marriage to Lisa Marie Presley.

"How long have you been in this place?" I asked.

"I don't remember," she said and quickly added, "but it's not so bad. Everything I need is here. Before the stores open in the morning, I do power walks with the outside people. Then I have a Cinnabon and wait for the stores to open."

"Don't you get bored shopping?" I asked.

"Oh no, I don't shop all the time. I have my blood pressure checked and I ice skate. Sometimes I go to a movie. A dentist just opened up on the third level, and there's a place outside Robinson's where I can get a massage.

"On weekends I go to a couple of weddings at the Chapel of Love. I love weddings."

"I suppose you can have the ceremony performed by an Elvis look-alike."

"You can have anything you want," she said. "Love mugs at $50 a pop, greatest moments from *All My Children* weddings flashed on the VCR, a wedding breakfast at Camp Snoopy, followed by a roller coaster ride. Before going on a honeymoon, the couple can claim their kids by former marriages at the mall's video game center."

"Haven't you ever been tempted to just bolt out of one of the exits?"

"What for?" she asked. "I'd never find my car. I'm safe in here. It's a life."

She was a wise woman.

I dreaded the idea of trying to find my car. In all my years of malling I have yet to come out of the same door as I went in. Quite simply this means I must circle the entire complex and go up and down every aisle before I return to a pay phone and report my car missing.

There is an army of us dragging up and down the acres of vehicles, our shopping bags scraping on the ground, our car keys in our teeth looking like frozen drool.

I hear a motor turn over. It gives me hope to keep going. Someone has found her car. If it happened today, it could happen tomorrow.

Then I see my car and squeeze through lines of vehicles to get to it. I look inside. It is clean and there is a trash bag dangling from a knob. There are no pine needles on the seat where I carried a Christmas wreath a year ago. *That's not my car!*

When I do discover it, there is good news and bad news: The clothes I just bought have gone out of style, but my car has become a classic.

Spiral garages are the worst. I use word association. If I am on the B level, I try to remember I got a B in phys ed in high school. L concourse will trigger the word "lucky," which is how I felt when a car pulled out of the spot just as I rounded the corner. Purple section was easy. Purple and orange are the colors of the Phoenix Suns, and my spot, 1028, is ten then doubled with an eight added.

When I return to my car my system has fallen apart. I go to the C level as it was my math grade in high school, on the F concourse because I was fortunate to get this spot, and the white section because that's what the

Phoenix Suns wear when they play on their home court.

I know you're wondering how all of this is going to tie in with our extinction. Stay with me, people. I just read a story that the end of the dinosaur era was possibly caused by a rapid decline in atmospheric oxygen in which wheezing animals roamed the earth too tired to compete for food. In short, they suffocated.

This is not unlike the thousands of weary shoppers who drag around mall parking lots looking for their cars and sucking up the exhaust of a thousand cars. After a few days, they become too tired to keep going and they can't breathe.

It's every woman's nightmare . . . dying while she still has a credit line on her Visa.

None of it is going to be a pretty sight to scientists looking for answers. A ghost town of signs flapping in the wind, rusted cars, litter, and an eerie recorded voice from within the mall that keeps repeating, "Elvis has just left the building."

Epilogue

The rain-swollen Salinas River went on a record rampage yesterday, spilling its banks, causing tens of millions of dollars in crop damage and forcing the evacuation of an estimated 5000 residents. The rising Salinas River floodwaters cut all remaining road and highway access yesterday to the Monterey Peninsula which had seen the Highway 1 bridge over the Carmel River collapse a day earlier.

Monterey County Herald, March 13, 1995

I started this book in Carmel. I had planned to finish it there, had there been electricity to run my typewriter, lights to illuminate my notes, and a bridge that would connect me to the library on the other side of the river.

It's probably just as well that the elements were against me. Once I am poised at my typewriter with the sea on one side and civilization on the other, I tend to sound like David Attenborough. I would have ended this book with some obvious parallel about how animals and humans are helpless when nature intervenes, and I couldn't resist leaving a message to the world on how if animals and humans didn't help one another, neither of us would survive.

But that's not what this book is all about.

It's about how close humans and animals are without even realizing it. I've seen every animal on these pages in Loehmann's community dressing room. I've seen the woman with the zebra print stretched across her fanny looking like she swallowed the gates to Buckingham Palace. I've zipped up a shopper with a panda waist in the back room who has chosen a black fur jumpsuit because it's 20 percent off.

I've been caught in a killer swarm of bargain hunters who hurt you to get an item with an "additional 20% off ticket price."

Every animal in this book—wild and domestic—is documented. They all exist. Either a scientist has researched them for years or I have had them to dinner. I have been fortunate to be able to combine my love of animals with people.

Every species fights against extinction. We do it by following the food and water supply, avoiding predators, and maintaining a balance of reproduction. But there is another dimension that enriches our lives: laughter. Without it, we'd never make it.

A few years ago, my husband and I were in Africa

going on game runs and photographing animal rumps. We would have preferred their faces, but it was their call.

As we stretched out on cots in a tent, the darkness was pierced by the shrill laugh of hyenas.

"They sure know how to have a good time," observed my husband.

"Either that or his wife just crammed her size 14 body into a size 3 nightgown with a Victoria's Secret label."

I know a sister when I hear one.